RALEIGH-DURHAM JOBS

Your source to jobs in the Triangle/Triad cities of Raleigh • Durham • Greensboro • Winston-Salem

Not just a vague, indiscriminate list of companies, but a **complete strategy** on how to uncover and utilize **every available source** to your advantage:

- Primary hiring companies in the Triangle and Triad region

- Employment agencies, both permanent an temporary

- Classified want ads

- Government positions

- Job fairs

- Professional and trade associations

- Network and support groups

- Free job assistance organizations

And more!

- Resume, cover letter, broadcast letters, and salary history preparation, with examples of each

- Interviewing strategies, including questions and answers

- Detailed company profiles, employment data and hiring procedures

RALEIGH-DURHAM

JOBS

featuring the

CAREER SEARCH SYSTEM

Steve Hines
Adam Bertolett

CareerSource Publications
Atlanta, Georgia

Published by CareerSource Publications, P O Box 52291, Atlanta, GA 30355.

Manufactured in the United States of America.

Graphics and cover design by West Paces Publishing, Atlanta, GA.

ISBN: 0-929255-16-X

YOUR INPUT IS VALUED,

AND WE WANT TO HEAR FROM YOU!

RALEIGH-DURHAM JOBS will be invaluable to you now, and we want future editions to be even more helpful. Your comments, suggestions and experiences help make that possible. If your comments or suggestions are incorporated in future editions, you will receive a complimentary copy.

Some topics to consider:

• Which of the source groups described in the Career Search System were most helpful in finding your job?

• Which ultimately secured your job?

• Which personnel agencies were most helpful? Least helpful?

• Are there any additional companies or industries you would like to see represented here?

• Are there any professional/trade associations or network groups you know that offer job assistance, and that are not included here?

• Any comments in general?

Mail your information to
CAREERSOURCE PUBLICATIONS
P O Box 52291, Atlanta, GA 30355.

Also available from CareerSource Publications:

THE JOB HUNT by Steve Hines
All you need to conduct a successful job search! Completely explains every part of the job search, including resume preparation, securing interviews, job networking, locating free help organizations, interview tips, and much, much more - even a self-analysis "What Am I Doing Wrong?" $12.95 + $2 postage/handling

THE CAREER SEARCH SYSTEM GUIDE TO
ATLANTA JOBS (ISBN 0-929255-15-1)
CHARLOTTE JOBS (ISBN 0-929255-09-7)
DALLAS/FT. WORTH JOBS (ISBN 0-929255-17-8)
Each book is $15.95 + $2 postage/handling.
Available in 1995: *Denver Jobs, Phoenix Jobs, Tampa Jobs*

JOBS SOUTHEAST
Quickly recovering from the recession, the Southeast offers innumerable employment opportunities. This guide pinpoints the 12 fastest growing cities in the SE and how to find employment in each one. Includes largest employers, network groups, local governments, etc. Available March, 1995.

JOB NETWORKING by Steve Hines
More job seekers find new employment through job networking than through all other sources combined! This step-by-step approach makes the process simple. $12.95 + $2 handling (ISBN #0-929255-14-3)

HOW TO GET A JOB ON A CRUISE SHIP By Don Kennedy
Make money and have fun! Learn step by step how to apply for and get one of the more than 30,000 jobs available every year on more than 100 cruise ships! Written by a former cruise staff member and officer for Royal Caribbean, Sitmar, Norwegian, and Carnival Cruise Lines. $10.95 + $2 handling (ISBN #0-929255-06-2)

For information and to order, contact
CAREERSOURCE PUBLICATIONS
P O Box 52291, Atlanta, GA 30355.
Or call (404) 262-7131; fax (404) 261-3169

TABLE OF CONTENTS

Chapters:

I. INTRODUCING THE CAREER SEARCH SYSTEM . . . page 11

II. STEP ONE: ORGANIZING YOUR JOB SEARCH . . . page 21
   Space . . . Equipment . . .Records . . . Time Management . . .
   Resources . . . Emotional Support Systems

III. STEP TWO: PREPARING YOUR RESUMES . . . page 29

   Part 1: The Written Word – The "Power Resume" . . . p. 31
   Part 2: The Oral Synopsis – The "30-Second Resume" . . p. 49
   Part 3: Business Cards . . . page 54

IV. STEP THREE: GET THAT INTERVIEW!. . . page 57

   Tool #1: Mass Mailing . . . page 68
   Tool #2: Direct Contact . . . page 72
   Tool #3: Classified Ads . . . page 80
   Tool #4: Permanent Employment Agencies . . . page 85
   Tool #5: Temporary Personnel Agencies . . . page 94
   Tool #6: Job Fairs . . . page 98
   Tool #7: Government. . . page 102
   Tool #8: Developing a Job Network . . . page 109
   Tool #9: Job Networking Groups . . . page 114
   Tool #10: Professional and Trade Associations . . . page 120
   Tool #11: Information Interview . . . page 126
   Tool #12: Public Agencies . . . page 134
   Tool #13: Privately Funded Organizations . . . page 136
   Tool #14: Useful Resources . . . page 138

V. STEP FOUR: INTERVIEWING TECHNIQUES . . . page 141
    Preparation . . . interviewing theory . . . "stress" interview . .
    . questions and answers . . . relocation . . . salary questions .
    . . "Why were you fired?" . . . interest questions . . . other
    considerations

VI. STEP FIVE: FOLLOW THROUGH . . . page 167

VII. SALARY NEGOTIATION . . . page 173

VIII. CORRESPONDENCE . . . page 181

        Cover Letters . . . page 183
        Broadcast Letters . . . page 187
        Thank-you Notes . . . page 188
        Salary Histories . . . page 189

IX. "WHAT AM I DOING WRONG?" . . . page 193
     Evaluating your job search . . . Energizing your marketing
     approaches . . . Interviewing mistakes

X. CONCLUSION . . . page 205

Appendices:

A. Sample Resumes, References, and Business Cards . . page 213

B. Sample Correspondence . . . page 233
    Cover Letters . . . Broadcast Letter . . . Salary Histories . . .
    Thank-you Notes

C. Detailed Profiles of Selected Companies . . . page 247

D. Personnel Agencies . . . page 285

E. Professional and Trade Associations . . . . page 291

F. Government Agencies . . . . page 299

for Lynnsey Hines,
as always

CHAPTER I

INTRODUCING THE
CAREER SEARCH SYSTEM

CHAPTER I

INTRODUCING THE

CAREER SEARCH SYSTEM

Good news: The cities of the Triangle and Triad region are a great
               place to live[1] and have thousands of job vacancies!
Bad news: The word is out, and thousands of job seekers have
               descended on the area.
Good news: There is a job here for you!

That's not just hype. There are indeed innumerable career opportunities available in the six cities that make up the Triangle and theTriad, but
the catch is how to find them. And that's not really a problem; it just
takes knowledge, a plan of action and the commitment to see the plan
through.

In the summer of 1970, I moved back South, ready to seek fame and
fortune in the business world. I had been teaching high school social
studies for the previous three years, and thus coddled in the world of
academia, I had no concept of what was in the "real world." I did not
know what jobs were out there, or what companies offered them, and
least of all, I didn't have the slightest idea how, where or what to do to
find my new career.

I wish I'd had a book like this!

---

[1] Money magazine (September 1994) rated Raleigh/Durham/Chapel Hill #1 place to
live in the US!

In the years since that summer, I have worked in personnel recruiting and placement. I have seen thousands of applicants struggle and stumble, trying to advance their careers – expending too much time, energy, and money, and going in pointless directions. Finding a job is just not that hard – if you know what to do!

But of course, most people don't. They have limited knowledge and resources from which to draw. I am always surprised at how otherwise extremely capable executives often produce the worst resumes and go on to interview poorly! Even corporate personnel administrators, whom one would expect to know what to do, appear to be just as much in the dark as everyone else.

The purpose of the **CAREER SEARCH SYSTEM** is to fill this vacuum of misinformation and lack of information, and to provide job seekers with the knowledge needed to successfully conduct a job search. This System represents more than twenty years of knowledge, gained almost entirely from that best teacher, experience. I have compiled the arcana, simplified and methodized it, and the result is the **CAREER SEARCH SYSTEM.**

What is the **CAREER SEARCH SYSTEM**? It is a step-by-step, hand-in-hand, practical guide to finding employment. Whether your objective is finding a new career, advancing your present career, or rebounding from a lay-off, the **CAREER SEARCH SYSTEM** will guide you to the best job available.

Within these ten chapters, you will discover all the information needed to obtain the right job in any of the cities in the Triad and Triangle. Outlined in detail are the who's, what's, how's, and when's, that will result in the job you want. Many sources are revealed that you probably never considered or knew existed. Even if you were aware of them, you may not have understood how to benefit from them.

The **CAREER SEARCH SYSTEM** will give you the tools you need to apply in your job search. You have only to use them, following the guidelines and directions.

There is one requirement: the firm commitment to find the job best suited for you. And that requirement will include work. You may hear many times, "Finding a job is a job in itself," and that is so true.

But since most of us would rather play than work, let's get into the spirit of job hunting with a little game, on pages 16 and 17.

(Refer to pp. 16 - 17)

Now back to the real world! I hope this exercise has shown you what is ahead in your job search. As this is a practical guide, I cannot help you in assessing your abilities or needs and wants. Once you have finished that, my system definitely will speed you the rest of the way.

The Career Search System

The **CAREER SEARCH SYSTEM** consists of five basic steps that will lead to job offers. Each step is discussed fully, describing in detail exactly what you should do.

Step #1 is organization. I am not a believer in creating work when none is required, but I have observed for many years that some basic organization is necessary for a successful job search. As your job hunt progresses, you will come to see the value of the systems and procedures I suggest and so I urge you not to rush into your campaign without this small amount of planning first.

Step #2 in your job search is to prepare your resume – not just a good resume, but a "better" resume: the "Power Resume." As you will read in the resume chapter, the first contact you make with a company is usually through your resume, and that first impression must be positive. Each section of the resume is discussed in detail, explaining how, when and why you use each, so that your resume will make the best first impression possible. Even if you plan to have a service prepare your resume, carefully read this chapter, so that you can give to the service the layout and standards you expect to be followed. Numerous examples are shown in Appendix A.

In addition to your written resume, you need two additional items:

1) You must develop a short, oral resume to use when you want to quickly relate your background and objective. How to prepare this "30-Second Resume" is also discussed as part of Step #2.

Start Here!
Move 1 space.

ASSESS YOUR ABILITIES:
Objectively—Move 2 spaces.
Non-objectively—Move 1 space.

STAY HERE UNTIL YOU TRY ANOTHER SOURCE

MARKET RESUME:
Move 1 space for
each marketing tool you use.

MOVE BACK & FORTH A WHILE, THEN MOVE 1 SPACE

2 sources are better than one, but use another source, then move 1 space.

Getting the Idea?
Use another source
and keep moving.

DITTO DITTO DITTO DITTO DITTO DITTO DITTO

JOB OFFER
YOU WIN!

Go to church and pray no one
else has both good interview
and good follow-up!

GO BACK TO START. GET HELP AND TRY AGAIN.

ASSESS NEEDS & WANTS
Realistically—Move 2 spaces.
Unrealistically—Move 1 space.

Stay Here Until You Come to Your Senses!

ORGANIZE
Skip Organization—
Move Back 1 Space

Organize equipment, time,
records & resources—
Move 1 Space

Organize emotional
support systems—
*Move 1 More
Space!*

PREPARE RESUME
**Ordinary Resume—Move 1 space.
"Power" Resume—Move 2 spaces.**

GET DEPRESSED
Wallow in self-pity!
Organize emotional
support systems—
Then Move On—

CONGRATULATIONS!
You Got an Interview
Prepared for interview—move 1 space.
Unprepared for interview—move back 12 spaces.

PREPARATION
Research only—
Move 1 space.
Research & Rehearse—
Move 2
spaces.

CLOSE
but we're not playing
horseshoes! Move
back 1 space.

GOOD INTERVIEW!
**FOLLOW-UP—Move 2 spaces.
NO FOLLOW-UP—Move 1 space.**

2) You need business cards to hand out in your networking efforts, as well as other opportunities when you don't have your written resume available. Examples of good business cards are included in Appendix A.

Now you are ready for **_Step #3_,** developing a marketing strategy to obtain interviews. If you have never been in sales and marketing before, you are now! Using a loose-leaf notebook to record your efforts and results, you will begin to develop contacts and sources in order to obtain interviews.

The System gives you far more sources from which to develop leads and interviews than you will probably use, but they are all there if you need them. Start with the ones that are the simplest and easiest for you, and if you are not satisfied with those results, use the others. The System even indicates which sources work best for different backgrounds, and so you can choose the one(s) best suited for you.

A major part of this marketing plan will include job networking. You probably have heard of this concept, but lacked the knowledge to make it work for you. Since more applicants find their jobs through some form of job networking than through all other sources combined, this approach is vital to your search. The **CAREER SEARCH SYSTEM** explains several networking procedures in complete detail, outlining exactly what you should do and say.

Once your marketing efforts are into full swing, you will begin to be invited for interviews. **_Step #4_** contains information on the preparation you must do before an interview, as well as the interview itself. Numerous questions, suggested answers, and the reasoning behind the questions and answers are discussed fully. If the very thought of interviewing makes you break out in a cold sweat, then relax. The **CAREER SEARCH SYSTEM** will have you well-prepared and will carry you through the interview with flying colors!

If you have always thought that once you finished the interview, your work was over, then think again! **_Step #5_** covers the follow-up procedure you should do after the interview, to give you an extra push. The "thank-you note" is discussed, as well as additional research and sources you can employ.

In addition to the five basic steps outlined in Chapters II – VI, additional chapters cover other information you may need in your job search.

"Chapter VII: Salary Negotiating" explains how salaries most often are determined by companies. When you should and should not consider negotiating is explained, and if you do wish to negotiate your salary offer, several suggestions and procedures are outlined.

Job-related correspondence is covered in Chapter VIII. The basic format for cover letters is given here, followed by the variations used for specific instances. What to include in your "thank-you note" is clarified, with suggestions for making yours stand out. How to report your salary information or write a salary history is also detailed. In addition, you can find numerous examples of these correspondences in Appendix B.

"What am I doing wrong?" is a question I frequently encounter, and I have the answers. Chapter IX discusses what to do should you find your job search at a standstill. I can help you evaluate your job search and pinpoint problems, then find the solutions. I have recommendations to energize your search and to help you avoid the common mistakes I so often observe.

Lastly, Chapter X concludes with a few more suggestions, even using rejection as an asset.

Conclusion

In the more than twenty years that I have been in personnel placement, I have dealt with hundreds of companies and their personnel representatives, interviewed thousands of applicants, and read tens of thousands of resumes. I stress my experience so you will understand that I know what is going on, in your mind and in the minds of companies, and to assure you that I know what I am talking about. I have encountered the problems you're facing many times, and I can help you find the solutions.

Step #1 in your job search is organization. Let's get started!

CHAPTER II

STEP ONE:

ORGANIZING YOUR JOB SEARCH

CHAPTER II:

Step One: Organizing Your Job Search

Getting Started

Every job will go smoother if you are organized, and this is definitely true of the job hunt. Before you write the first word on your resume or make your first phone call, you must be organized.

Organize your space. If at all possible, you should have a designated work area with a desk, phone, and the supplies you will need. Working off of the kitchen table is not satisfactory and you will quickly see why. Also, a small, two-drawer file cabinet and several file folders will be very helpful in keeping your information organized and easy to find. In other words, set up an in-house office, just as you would have at your job.

Organize your equipment. Have your phone convenient to your work area. Buy a telephone answering machine, if you don't already own one; they are relatively inexpensive, and using one will prevent you from missing any calls for information or interviews.[1]

---

[1]My pet peeve has become people who leave a message on my phone recorder, but speak so rapidly and/or enunciate so poorly that I cannot decipher the information, especially their phone number. When leaving messages, always repeat your name and phone number so that the receiver will have no difficulty returning your call.

If you can afford one or have access to one, a fax machine (or fax modem with your computer) also will be very useful. I have observed that many companies are advertising that you can fax your resume instead of mailing it. You also can fax your resume to personnel agencies, both permanent and temporary, for faster consideration. [1]

A typewriter is a bare necessity, but you really need access to a computer and laser printer. With a computer, you easily can personalize your correspondence and resume to fit each situation, as well as store information for later reference. If you do not own a computer, try to locate a free source before you lease time or rent one. For example, many state employment offices have computers available for job seekers. Public libraries and college placement offices are other sources to check.[2]

Have business cards printed with your name, contact data, and your employment objective or expertise, but do not attempt to condense your resume onto this small card (see Appendix A for examples); you will use these cards extensively during your search, especially when job networking.

Organize your records. One of the complaints I often hear from job changers is that their present company requires too much paperwork. Companies don't require this work just to keep their employees busy, but rather they see the need to keep accurate and timely records, for use now and to refer to later. I personally do not enjoy keeping records, and yet I have learned over the years that I must.

I have kept the volume of paperwork you need for your job search to a minimum, so don't short-cut the little I have included. As your job search progresses, you will see the need for each item.

You will need a loose-leaf notebook with eight dividers and lots of paper to record your activities. Label the dividers with these topics:

---

[1] If you do fax your resume, I urge you also to mail a copy, since many older fax machines use a coated paper that fades and disintegrates after a time.

[2] If you are not computer literate, now is an ideal time to learn at least the basics. Every company and every discipline is becoming more dependent on computers, and your lack of computer ability will severely hinder your career. Consider taking free or low cost classes through a local college or adult education program.

- Time organizer

- Company "cold calls"

- Newspaper ads

- Personnel agency contacts

- Professional contacts

- Personal contacts

- Professional associations

- Information interviews

Organize your time. How much time can you spend on your job search? If you are currently employed, you must budget your time wisely, conducting your search in the evenings, weekends, and during the workday when possible. If you are unemployed, you should plan to spend at least 40 hours per week in your search, and you should plan your schedule just as effectively as you would in your employment. Use the example illustrated at the beginning of Chapter IV, called "Weekly Timetable," or some other time organizer.

During your unemployment, strive to maintain the same schedule to which you have become accustomed. Don't allow yourself to wallow in bed every morning, or you will be wasting valuable time. In addition, when you begin your new employment, you will have difficulty readjusting to the work regimen.

If you find yourself with extra time, use it constructively by establishing new contacts through volunteer work (see Job Networking in Chapter IV), enrolling in career enhancement classes, or acquiring certification in your field. Now is an excellent time to study up on new industry trends and advancements, especially computer-related developments. Include in your resume that you are currently attending these job-related classes; companies will be impressed that you are using your time wisely and learning additional skills.

If you have been a member of a health spa, continue your workouts just as before. Exercise is an excellent way to cope with stress.

Organize your resources. Files, phone books, and other reference materials should be within easy reach. Keep a copy of **Raleigh-Durham Jobs** close at hand, since you will refer to it often. Think of this book as a workbook, similar to the ones you used in school. You should underline or highlight passages, write in the margins, fold down the edges of pages you want to refer to later – anything that will help you derive the most from the information contained here. In fact, by the end of your job search, this book should be thoroughly worn out.

Support Systems

There is one more item to organize, and this is by far the most important. If you learn nothing else from this book or only follow one of my suggestions, let it be this one: Don't attempt a job search at all until you have organized and have in place your psychological and emotional support systems.

I just spoke with an applicant who has 15 years experience in commercial real estate. Unfortunately, that field is very depressed currently and his job search has now stretched into seven months. His exact words to me were, "I sit across from my wife at breakfast every morning and I know she is thinking 'What is wrong with him?'." Of course, what he really meant to say was "What is wrong with me?"

Even in the best of economic times, conducting a job search is a highly traumatic and stressful endeavor. In the recent recession and slow recovery, the <u>average</u> length of time required to find new employment has stretched into many months. Even worse, in the past few months I have spoken with too many job seekers who have been looking for more than a year.

Maintaining a positive attitude through this most trying of times is painfully difficult, and you must recognize your need for the support of close friends and family, including your children. Let them know what you are doing every step of the way and what they can do to help you. Tell them of your frustrations and anxieties, fears and depression. Those are normal feelings and nothing to be ashamed of or suppressed.

Unfortunately, I have witnessed too many divorces and dissolutions of friendships that resulted from this stressful period. Open your lines of communication and keep them open at all times. You will be pleasantly surprised to discover how understanding and helpful your support systems can be.

In addition, you should keep them informed of the positive aspects of your job search – your progress and up-coming interviews, of your research and what you have learned. Many of these experiences will be very interesting and you will enjoy sharing them with your friends.

Join organizations, both those pertaining to your profession as well as non-profit charity associations. Become active and volunteer your time. This will give you needed diversions and new purposes, and also introduce you to another set of contacts, some of whom may be helpful in your job search.

Prepare yourself, too, by adjusting your attitude. Nothing can ruin a beautiful, sunny day faster than receiving a rejection letter in the mail. Accept the fact that you will be experiencing some let-downs and – yes – rejections, and don't be overwhelmed. When you begin to feel yourself slipping into a depression, that is the signal to pull out your emotional support systems and get back on track.

On the positive side, this time can be an opportunity for reflection, a time when you can sit back and evaluate your life and career direction. Are you really happy with your current occupation? What would you like to do differently? What are your goals? Most importantly, what are your priorities? What is important to you, in your personal life as well as your career?

All of this organization is vital to a successful job search, as you will come to see. Best of all, remember you are far ahead in the career search game already: You bought and are reading *Raleigh-Durham Jobs*!

CHAPTER III

STEP TWO:

PREPARING YOUR RESUMES AND BUSINESS CARDS

Part 1: The "Power Resume"

Part 2: The "30-Second Resume"

Part 3: Business Cards

CHAPTER III

Step Two: Preparing Your Resumes and Business Cards

Part 1: The Written Word – The "Power Resume"

It's not what you know, but how you present it. Let me explain.

I recently ran a small, classified ad in the local newspaper for a manufacturing plant manager. In response to that one short ad, I received more than 100 resumes; a larger ad would probably have elicited many more. Obviously, I did not have time to interview all of these applicants, or even to call them all. Many of them had the right background and experience, so what criteria did I use in deciding which to interview first? I used the same test that every other recruiter uses: the quality of the resume.

And what happens to the applicants with the poor resumes? I don't know, since I never call them!

Thus, you see that a resume has both positive and negative potential, and we can draw two conclusions regarding the resume:

1) A resume can secure you an interview, which ultimately may result in a job.

2) But a resume also can *prevent* you from getting an interview, and thus you will never have the opportunity to show why you should be employed there.

The importance of a good resume cannot be overstressed. Even if you have exactly the right background the company is seeking; even if you can interview perfectly; and even if you would make an ideal employee for the company, you will never get in the door if the company's first impression of you is negative, based on a poorly prepared resume.

Wow! Did you ever think that one sheet of paper could have so much power over your life and career?

But not only does your resume need to be "good," it also needs to be "better," that is, better than your competition. Imagine reviewing 100 resumes for just one opening! In order to peruse that many resumes in a cost-effective time frame, I tend to scan through the pile and pull out the ones that look the most appealing and are able to grab my attention quickly . Since a positive impression of the applicant has already been established, these "better" resumes receive more attention and sooner. The others never even may be read.

This chapter will explain how to write a "better" resume and how to use its power to your advantage. In short, you will learn how to write the "Power Resume."

What makes up a "Power Resume"? There are many factors involved, and we will cover them in detail. In addition, numerous examples are given in Appendix A. First, however, let's discuss what a resume is.

Simply stated, a resume is

"A short summary of your positive qualifications for employment."

Now let's analyze that definition.

Short: Most applicants need only a one-page resume, or two pages at the absolute most. And yet too many job-seekers feel that a short resume implies a lack of experience, and conversely, a long one suggests a well-qualified applicant. Nothing could be further from the truth. In fact, a lengthy resume suggests a verbose egoist, unable to discern the important from the irrelevant!

OK, maybe that's a bit severe. Truthfully, many job-seekers are probably not aware of what should and should not be in a resume. Perhaps that is why you are reading this. Bear in mind that personnel departments receive many, many resumes, and I assure you that from my own experience and from discussions with corporate recruiters, long resumes are seldom read. On the contrary, concise resumes get the most attention.

While on this subject, here's a bit of crazy logic: I recently interviewed a manager with a three-page resume. When I asked him if he ever read the three-page resumes he received, he immediately said "No!" He then went on to tell me that nevertheless, he was certain other managers would read his!

Summary: This is a resume, not your autobiography, and it should sum up only information germane to your job search. It should not include irrelevant information, such as your appointment to the college homecoming court or being selected "Most Eligible Bachelor," and do not include a photograph.

Your: This is *your* resume, not anyone else's. Do not mention the names and background of your family, spouse, and children, or the name of your supervisor. (Incidentally, I once had an applicant rejected for an interview because his resume referred to "my lovely wife Lorain and our two adorable children, Mark and Susie.")

Positive: "Accentuate the positive," as the old song goes. A resume should emphasize achievements, accomplishments, honors, and awards, and omit any negatives. You may even wish to include a brief summary section, highlighting your best assets. Use positive wording, creating an up-beat image of yourself. If you were ever fired from a job, a resume is definitely not the place to reveal it.

Qualifications: Education, experience, personal data, references.

Employment: The finish line!

Preparation

Now that you understand what a resume is and what it can do, you can begin to assemble yours, by obtaining the necessary subjective and objective data. Objective data is listed below, but depending on your experience and job goal, you may not use all of it. In particular, the information on your college education will become less important as you gain more career-related work experience. Employment that occurred more than ten years ago should be included only very briefly, in favor of your more recent experience, which should be discussed more fully.

In general, this is what you need to compile:

1) Address and phone number (permanent and temporary, if applicable)

2) College information, including

- graduation dates (month and year)

- grade point average (major and overall) and/or class ranking

- honors, achievements, elective offices, etc.

- percent of college expenses earned

- activities, including sports, clubs and professional organizations

- for recent grads, career-related courses taken or scheduled

3) Career-related seminars, courses, and special training

4) Professional distinctions, honors, achievements, awards

5) Hobbies and interests

6) Activities, including membership in professional organizations and civic associations

7) Employment data, including

- brief description of your company(s) and its products/services, if not generally known to the public

- title or functional title

- dates of employment

- duties, responsibilities, and descriptions

- accomplishments, awards, sales quotas, distinctions, etc.

8) Career-related experience, other than through direct employment.

Now is the time to plan whom you will use for references, and confirm with them. Three references are sufficient, probably one professional, one personal, and one academic (for recent grads) or former employer. (Incidentally, we have further plans for using your references to aid in your job search. This will be discussed later in "Chapter IV: Marketing Strategies.")

In addition to that objective data, you need to assess your skills and qualifications, strengths and weaknesses. Be honest with yourself and answer the following:

- Why should XYZ Corporation interview (and maybe hire) me?

- What do I have that other applicants may not?

- What do I do best? Worst?

- What are my best developed talents (judgment, communications, work relationships, decision-making, etc.)?

- What are the most important achievements and accomplishments of my life and career?

These answers are important in understanding your employment assets. Start planning how you might incorporate them into your resume.

Format

35

There is no one universal format used by all job-seekers, but rather basic sections that can be worded and assembled to fit each person's background. The information I have outlined here is very general in nature and will result in a functional/chronological resume, the type most commonly accepted. However, under certain circumstances, you may wish to use a topical format, which will be discussed later.

Most importantly, as you write your descriptions, keep in mind why you are writing this resume: to impress a potential employer and gain an interview. Thus, you want to include not only your basic qualifications, but also distinctions and achievements that put you ahead of your peers.

Name and address: At the top of your resume, place your name, address, and phone number. Type your name in all capitals and use boldface in larger-size type, if available. Professional certifications, such as C.P.A., should be included on the line with your name (JOHN A. DOE, C.P.A.). If you have a temporary address (*e.g.*, a student) you can use that address and include a permanent address at the bottom or elsewhere, noting when it will be effective. If you are moving soon, you can use either your old or new address and phone number; just be certain that you always can be contacted by prospective employers. Needless to say, update your resume with the new address as soon as possible. If you feel comfortable receiving phone calls at work, you may include both your home and work phone numbers.

Objective: If you include an Objective, this will be the first section, after your name and address. If you are applying for a specific opening or in a specific industry, tailor your objective to fit. Remember, however, that if your resume states a specific objective (*e.g.*, sales) and you are applying for another (*e.g.*, management), you likely will not be considered. Thus, if you are not so sure about a specific objective, you can construct it to be more open in nature. A better alternative used by many applicants is to prepare two or more resumes with different objectives, and use the one most appropriate. Or you can simply omit the objective all together, and open your resume with a Summary paragraph. In practice, I find that I tend to omit the Objective more and more often, in favor of a Summary section (described below) and a very personalized cover letter, and that is what I suggest you do also.

Summary: The purpose of a Summary section is twofold:

1) Summarize your abilities

2) Highlight your qualifications that propel you ahead of other applicants.

A summary paragraph is optional, but it can be very effective, especially if you have some short, important data you wish the reader to see first, as an enticement to read further. Do not defeat its purpose by making it too long and thus lose its impact.

The Summary can be used with or without an Objective, or you can incorporate the Objective within this section. It should be very positive and up-beat, with an emphasis on abilities and achievements. Here are three examples, and more are included on the sample resumes in Appendix A:

> Proven success in solution-oriented Sales and active Sales Management. Consistently promoted or recruited as a result of outstanding sales performance. Assembled highly effective and cohesive sales teams.

> Recent college graduate in Business Administration with proven record of initiative and accomplishment. Completely financed all education costs through full-time employment, thus gaining five years of business experience. Seeking Management Development Program utilizing practical experience and academics.

> Accounting/Finance graduate with more than four years accounting and auditing experience. Thorough knowledge of federal tax policies and procedures. Experienced with both manual and automated invoice systems, using Lotus 1-2-3 software. Seeking position as either Staff Accountant or Accounting Department Manager.

Whether you use an Objective or Summary section, or both, or neither, be certain your resume has direction and focus. Don't try to make your resume so open that it seems as though you have no idea what career you are pursuing. Recruiters will assume that is exactly the case and will pass over your resume for one more focused.

Education: You can use either Education or Employment as your next section, depending on which is the stronger or more important. For example, recent grads with limited or no relevant experience will place the Education section first. However, if you were a co-op student or intern, or have some other good business experience, list that first and Education next. More experienced applicants will generally place the Employment section ahead. An exception to this is that experienced applicants with a degree from a highly regarded institution could list Education first. As you gain more experience, the Education section will continue to shrink, as the Employment section grows.

For the recent college graduate with limited career-related experience, academics will be paramount and thus will incorporate a large part of the resume. State the name of your college, the type of degree you will be receiving, major and minor concentrations, and month and year you expect to graduate. If you had a high Grade Point Average (above 3.0 on a 4.0 scale) and/or graduated in the top one-half of your class, include that information. Then list a few relevant courses that you have taken or plan to take. Earning a large part of your tuition and expenses shows initiative and should be mentioned. Definitely include honors, activities, and elected positions. If you have more than one degree to include, list the most recent first.

Applicants with relevant work experience will list most of the same education information, eliminating less important data with each new job and subsequent resume. Course titles will be the first to be eliminated, followed by activities and minor honors. For about ten years, continue to include a good Grade Point Average, important honors, and elected positions. By then, your recent achievements will be more indicative of your abilities.

If you are not a college graduate, I suggest you omit the Education section entirely, although you can include a reference to your academics in the Personal section, such as "Attended ABC University for three years, majoring in Business Administration," or "Currently enrolled at ABC University, pursuing a Bachelor's degree in Marketing. Graduation expected in June 1996."

After you have listed your academic institutions, then include relevant seminars and courses taken, and the dates. Also, include any professional certifications (C.P.A., Professional Engineer, etc.) or awards gained through additional studies, and the dates bestowed. However, do not include certifications from previous careers that are not germane to your current job search; for example, omit references to real estate courses, if you are no longer pursuing that career.

Employment: Note: You may call this section "Experience" if you wish, especially if you are including experience gained through non-employment (*e.g.*, volunteer work), temporary assignments, or part-time jobs.

All potential employers want to see some work experience, even for recent grads, and the more successful and relevant it is to your job objective, the better your chances of securing employment. List your job title, company name, dates of employment, and description of job duties. That seems simple enough, but since it is the most important part of your resume, it must be perfect. Follow these guidelines, and refer to Appendix A for examples:

1) Use reverse chronology (last job first).

2) Be concise, and thus hold your resume to one page, if possible, and never more than two.

3) Don't get bogged down in details and don't feel you must include everything you have done. Save something for the interview!

4) Titles sometimes can be misleading; use functional, descriptive titles when necessary. For example, I recently prepared a resume for an individual who was managing the company's entire personnel function, although his title was only Personnel Administrator; I used Personnel Director as his title, to emphasize the scope of his responsibilities.

5) Be certain to include management and supervisory responsibilities.

6) Emphasize accomplishments, awards, and achievements. Underline and/or use boldface on the most important.

7) List your last or current job date as "present," even if you are no longer with the company, unless many months have passed since your departure. That may sound strange, but it is an accepted practice, since revealing your unemployment raises questions which probably could be explained best during an interview. However, you can explain your employment status in your cover letter, if you wish, or wait for your first contact with a company representative.

8) The most recent experience generally should have the longest description; experience more than ten years ago can be combined for brevity.

9) Percentages are usually more easily understood than exact figures, since the relevance of large and small amounts varies from industry to industry. Unless you are certain your readers will understand and/or be impressed with your figures, consider using percentages instead.

10) Do not list your reasons for leaving an employer, unless it makes a very positive point or explains several recent job changes.

11) Do not use acronyms or arcana that may be unfamiliar to most readers.

12) Include a brief description of your company(s) and its products/services, if most readers might not be familiar with it.

13) Numbers less than 10 should be written out.

14) Do not state your salary on the resume. However, some classified ads may request your current salary or a salary history, which can be included in your cover letter or on a separate page. (See "Chapter VIII: Correspondence.")

15) Since many companies shy away from individuals who have been self-employed, I suggest you avoid direct references to that. For example, you could describe your job title as "General Manager," rather than "Owner."

16) Use mostly "non-sentences" without a pronoun subject, and avoid using personal pronouns. Definitely do not write in the third person and avoid using the passive voice.

Personal: This section is optional and the current trend now is to omit it, especially for more experienced applicants. The reason is that your personal data should not effect your job performance, and therefore it should not be a consideration in your job application. In addition, some personal information could lend itself to possible discrimination, legal and illegal.[1]

Frankly, I prefer the resumes I receive to have a Personal section, since it often can yield a more complete picture of the candidate. Nevertheless, I generally do not include one on the resumes I prepare, in deference to the above reasoning.

However, if you have some special information to convey that you feel is relevant to your job objective, or if you simply feel that the information will yield a more thorough appraisal of you, you should include a Personal section.

If you do decide to add a Personal section to your resume, this is some of the information that may be included: birth date (not age, since that may change during your job search), marital status, height/weight, and if you are available for travel. Unless there are absolutely, positively no circumstances under which you will consider relocation, I urge you to add that you are open for relocation; the reasons for including this are explained in "Chapter V: Interviewing Techniques."

Do not mention potential negatives (*e.g.*, obesity) or restrictions (*e.g.*, geographic). Some states restrict including age, and you may omit that if you feel it could be a handicap, and the same is true for marital status. Never state your race or religion, but do include citizenship status, if you sense it may be in question.

Next mention a few hobbies and interests (reading, sports, music, etc.), that you are actively pursuing and that can be used to "break the ice" during an interview. (Then be ready to discuss them; for example, if you list reading as an interest, be prepared for the question, "What have you read lately?") If you are multilingual, add that here; if you are not quite fluent, you can describe yourself as "proficient." If you have several years of college, but did not graduate, you may mention that here. If you have excellent career experience and have decided to stress that in lieu of a separate Education section, you should list your college

---

[1] What is "legal discrimination"? You may be surprised to learn that not all discrimination is banned by federal statutes. In most states, including Georgia, you may be denied employment based on your appearance (although morbid obesity may be covered by the Americans with Disabilities Act), marital status, sexual preference, foreign citizenship, or geographic restrictions. Even discrimination addressed by law often has exceptions.

degree here. Finally, include memberships in professional associations and your civic involvements; however, do not include more than three, lest your priorities be called into question.

References: You may end your resume with "References available on request." If you get to the bottom of your resume and will have to crowd to add this final sentence, either omit it or include it as the last sentence in your Personal section.

I recently read an article that described this closing line as "utterly useless" and suggested omitting it, and I also have discussed this with several professional resume writers whose opinions I respect. Frankly, I agree that it is stating the obvious – of course you will have references! – but it is also a good method of saying "The End" in more tactful terms, and it can be a good balance in your layout. Whether you include it or not is your decision; your resume will not rise or fall on that sentence.

Do not list your references on the resume, but do prepare a separate "References" page to have should they be requested of you; see Appendix A for examples.

Topical Format

As I stated earlier, the functional/chronological resume is the most widely used and accepted form because it is simple and easy to understand. Under certain circumstances, however, the topical format may be better suited for your use.

The topical format differs from the functional/chronological format in that it includes an Experience section, either in addition to or in lieu of the Employment section. It can be especially helpful when you are changing careers or re-entering the job market, and want to emphasize knowledge you have gained that is relevant to your new job objective. It also can be used to summarize what might otherwise be a very lengthy resume by combining many jobs into skill categories. And finally, it can be used simply to emphasize certain points or skills you feel important. Several examples of this format are shown in Appendix A.

I have begun to use more often a variation of this format, combining it with the functional/chronological. When doing so, I generally choose the two or three skills that best summarize my applicant's experiences or abilities, and include them under the heading "Qualifications." For example, I did a Communications Specialist's resume by summarizing her experiences in Marketing, Public Relations, and Copywriting, and then listing her employment and a very brief description of the responsibilities of each position.

Synopsis/Amplification Format

This resume version consists of a synopsis page that includes all the basic information and sections, but with no details. The details of employment and experience are placed on a separate page, called an "Amplification." I receive these occasionally, and they are acceptable. I really don't recommend them, however, because invariably they get too long and so bogged down in detail that they are difficult to read, not to mention boring. As I have stated before, save the details for an interview, when you have the opportunity to explain personally your experiences.

The Finished Product

In Appendix A, I have included many examples of excellent resumes, and I have tried to illustrate as many diverse situations and backgrounds as possible. But because each person's background is unique, do not try to copy too closely any example given. There are many acceptable variations of the basic format, and if you keep in mind your purpose in constructing a resume, you can vary the format to fit your needs.

In typing your resume, you should not use the old-model electric typewriter of many years ago. Much better results now can be obtained with an electronic typewriter/word processor with a laser or letter-quality printer. Better still, using a computer with a word processing program and a laser printer will give your resume the appearance of being professionally typeset. Do not use a dot-matrix printer.

As this is a resume, not a sales brochure, do not adopt any format that looks "gimmicky." Use separate sheets of standard size 8 1/2" x 11" paper, printed on one side only.

After you have finished typing, carefully proofread for errors and misspellings. Ask two or three friends to read it also, for suggestions and further proofreading.

When you are satisfied with your product, have copies made at a local quick-print shop; it's probably cheaper than you think and the

Your resume must <u>always</u> . . .

- Be focused
- Emphasize accomplishments and achievements
- Be concise and to-the-point
- Appear neat and clean

Your resume must <u>never</u> . . .

- Seem too vague or misdirected
- Run more than two pages
- Look like a brochure
- Include too much detail
- Be typed on an old manual typewriter

copies generally will look better than those produced on the standard office photocopier. Choose a good quality of cream, light beige, or buff-colored paper for best results, although plain white is certainly acceptable. Do not use green, pink, or any other brightly colored paper. Also, do not use parchment paper, which does not photocopy well and because of its density, does not fax well either.

Buy extra blank pages to use for cover letters, and envelopes that match your stationery. Ask the printer (or your resume service, if you are having it prepared for you) if they can match your resume's letter-head (name and contact data) onto the blank, cover letter pages. That is an optional touch, but the matching letterhead on your resume and cover letter will appear more professional and appealing. Above all, be certain the resume is neat and clean; remember, it represents you.

And finally, here are a few common grammatical mistakes I have observed through the years on the resumes I have reviewed:

1) Without question, the most frequently misspelled word on resumes is "liaison," probably misspelled on a third of the resumes I receive. Another word often misspelled and misused is "Bachelor." It does not contain a "t" (batchelor), and the degree is a Bachelor of Whatever or a Bachelor's degree, not a Bachelor's of Whatever. The same is true of Master's degrees.

2) The most commonly misspelled (and overused!) abbreviation is "etc." (not ect.), and note the correct punctuation of the abbreviation "et al." (a period after "al," not "et").[2]

3) The most common punctuation errors I observe are in the misuse of periods, commas, semicolons, and colons, and the misplacement of quotation marks. The correct usage of these punctuation marks is generally misunderstood, and unless you are positive you have used them correctly, I advise you to check with a grammar reference book. Three primary examples are these:

---

[2] Incidentally, the correct punctuation for foreign words used in print is to underline or italicize them. However, the Latin abbreviations "etc." and "et al." have become so commonly accepted that we no longer treat them differently. Other foreign words, such as *cum laude,* should continue to be underlined or italicized.

- Commas and periods are always placed *inside* quotation marks, and the reverse is true for colons and semicolons. The placement of question marks and exclamation points varies, depending on the usage. (Now that you know this, notice how often it is done incorrectly!)

- The word "however" is preceded by a *semicolon*, not a comma, when used as a conjunctive adverb, separating clauses of a compound sentence; however, a comma is correct when using "however" as a simple conjunction or adverb. If this sounds confusing – and it does to me! – just notice how I have correctly used "however" throughout this book.

- Colons should be used at the end of a complete sentence, not a phrase.

4) Other frequent grammatical mistakes are inconsistencies in verb tense and in parallel structure.

If you still have questions regarding correct word usage, spelling, or grammar, you can call the Grammar Hot Line at one of the two participating North Carolina colleges listed below. This free service is staffed by professors who work the hot line on a volunteer basis between their regular schedule of classes. If your question cannot be immediately answered, the staffer will research the information and call you back.

Methodist College in Fayetteville
(919) 488-7110
Call Monday - Friday, 8:00 am - 5:00 pm

East Carolina University in Greenville
(919) 757-6728 or 757-6399
Call Monday - Thursday, 8:00 am - 4:00 pm; Friday 8:00 am - 3:00 pm; or Tuesday and Thursday evenings form 6:00 pm - 9:00 pm

Conclusion

Now let's go back to the question I posed earlier, "What makes up a 'Power Resume'?" The resumes in Appendix A are all good examples of "Power Resumes." Observe that they all follow these guidelines:

1) Proper layout

2) Concise, preferably one page and never more than two pages

3) Attention to detail, especially spelling, grammar and neatness

4) Emphasis on the positive (accomplishments, honors, awards and achievements)

5) Relevance to your job objective.

Thus the answer to the question is simple: Follow the outline and guidelines presented here, and you will have composed your own "Power Resume." My knowledge on the subject is first-hand, having read many thousands of resumes, written at least a thousand more, and consulted with other personnel recruiters to obtain their input as well. Thus, you can rest assured that your better and more powerful resume will get the best results possible.

P. S.

Now that you know what is involved in preparing your own resume, you may be concerned that it is too difficult and time-consuming for you, and you may be planning to have a professional resume service prepare it for you. Considering some of the home-made products I receive, I might encourage that also – but with definite reservations and qualifications.

In the past, I have been hesitant to recommend the use of resume services, because I have seen so many poor results. In fact, I recently discussed this with the former Director of Employment for a major southeastern corporation, and who is now a training consultant. We were talking about resumes – specifically, the bad ones – and we agreed that some of the worst were "professionally" prepared.

Let me quickly add, however, that although I most remember those bad examples, I have also reviewed many excellent resumes that were prepared by resume services. A good, experienced resume service can be extremely helpful; just be careful with your choice. Insist on editorial approval and be certain it meets our standards before you accept it. Ask the background and experience of the person who will be preparing your resume, and request to see actual copies of recent work. Show them some of the samples I have included in Appendix A, to use as a pattern for your resume.

The best of these services will have a personal computer with a laser printer that can do italics, boldface and variable-size type. Excellent results can be obtained, however, using an electronic typewriter or word processor with proportional pitch and the ability to justify right and left margins. You should not pay to have your resume printed on the standard electric typewriter of many years ago.

Although the layout and appearance are important, the paramount factor is the content of your resume. You can help in this preparation (and probably save money) by composing most of the content of your resume beforehand, and simply have the service do the re-typing and lay-out correctly.

Whatever you decide, remember that this resume represents *you*. If you have the time and feel competent, use the information I have outlined and make your own resume. It's really not as difficult as you might imagine. Otherwise, pay to have it prepared for you, but be satisfied that it is an accurate depiction of you, and that it does you justice.

Keep your resume current!

Within a few weeks of your new employment, update your resume, and always have an updated version available. Every time you receive a promotion or achieve some distinction, add it to your resume. If you are doing a good job, the word will get out, and sooner or later someone will approach you with a possible new job!

Part 2

The Oral Synopsis:
The "30-Second Resume"

How many times have you been at a party, seminar, or other meeting when someone turned to you and said, "Tell me about yourself," or "What do you do?" or "What is your background?" What did you answer?

"Well, I was an accountant, but now I'm between jobs," or "I used to be an accountant, but was laid off. Do you know of any job openings?" Worse yet, did you ramble on for several minutes and bore your listener so badly that he/she was wishing to be in another room, another place, another time?

Wouldn't it be great if you had a short, prepared answer that covered your background highlights and job objective, and still kept your listener's attention?

During your job search, you will encounter many networking opportunities when you will be called upon to relate your qualifications and objectives. Some of these situations you will have created through your specific networking efforts, but there also will be other times when someone simply will turn to you and ask, "What do you do?"

You should be prepared for these opportunities with a short, oral synopsis of your background and career objective. Since you may have

49

only a few moments of your listener's time, you need an answer that will quickly stress the most important factors you want your listener to know while you have his/her undivided attention. You cannot hope to relate all of your background, experiences, and achievements at once, but rather you will reveal just enough of your background to hold your listener's interest and hopefully lead to further dialogue.

What you need is a "30-Second Resume."

I recently attended a seminar in which the speaker commented that the average American executive has an attention span of approximately thirty seconds! I do not know the accuracy of his source, but that generally confirmed my suspicions and experiences. Perhaps if you will be honest about it, that may be true for you too!

When I receive phone calls from job seekers asking for advice, I always ask, "What is your background?" or "Tell me about yourself," and their answer reveals much of what is right or wrong in their job search. If they are unable to relay quickly and concisely their background, or if they ramble on until I cut them off, then I know what they should do first: they must compose their "30-second resume."

Composing your "30-Second Resume"

When writing your "30-second resume," bear in mind when and how you will use it, remembering its two primary purposes:

1) to relay only the most important facets of your background

2) to arouse enough interest to lead to further dialogue.

Note that its purpose is not to include all the information you want to relate, and since you want to involve your listener in dialogue, you should keep your discourse upbeat and non-technical.

What should you include? First answer these questions:

1) What are the requirements for the job I am seeking?

2) What in my background fits those requirements?

Armed with that information, you can begin to separate relevant material from information that can be discussed later. Then plan how you will capsulate the most relevant material into a very short time span – approximately 30 seconds. If your listener seems interested in hearing more, you can elaborate and give details then. But first, you must get his/her attention with your "30-second resume."

Preparing this oral resume may take as much time as your written one, and it is equally as important. Probably the worst mistake job seekers make with their written resume is making it too long and detailed, boring the reader and losing his/her attention. I assume you already know that the purpose of a resume is not to get you a job, but to arouse just enough interest to obtain an interview.

The same is true regarding your oral resume. Keep it short and relevant to your job objective, saying just enough to show you are qualified and to keep your listener's attention. What would you want to hear if you were the listener? What can you say that will arouse interest and perhaps lead to further discussion?

Most importantly, plan this well in advance and then rehearse it aloud or with a friend. Here are some factors to consider:

> *Job objective:* In as few words as possible, explain the field or type of job you are seeking. Probably this should be the first item in your oral resume, but you also can explain your qualifications first and then show how it fits into your career plans.

> *Education and training:* Some professions emphasize academics, and if you have the right degree, you should mention it. (For example, a science degree may be helpful in a pharmaceutical or chemical sales position; a degree in industrial management is good preparation for a manufacturing management position; a marketing MBA is usually vital to a staff marketing position; etc.) Familiarity with computer hardware and software programs is becoming a necessity in most professions, and you probably will want to indicate your proficiency. Certification is nearly always an important asset and should be stressed. Career-related seminars and training programs also may be added, if they are well-known.

> *Skills:* Some examples are good communicator, self-motivated, well-organized, aggressive, etc. Keep in mind that you may be called upon to give specific instances showing how you exem-

plify these characteristics, so be prepared with some good illustrations.

Accomplishments and achievements: This is an integral part of both your written and oral resumes, and must always be included. Of what in your life and career are you the proudest? Choose the most important one or two and mention them. Remembering that corporations are all "bottom-line"-oriented, you should also stress any increases in revenue or decreases in expenses due to your efforts.

Prior employment: If you seek to advance your current career path, then your past and current employment may be the most important information to stress. Condense it into a few sentences, stating job titles or descriptive titles and the responsibilities you have had.

Other experience: If your objective is to change careers, mention specific experiences that relate to your new field. For example, if outside sales is your objective, stress your familiarity with the product line, through experience, academics, or whatever. Volunteer experience and civic involvement may have given you some experience relevant to your new career. Prior employment could have given you some transferable skills or knowledge.

I realize that this may be an enormous amount of information to condense into thirty-or-so seconds, but you must.

If you still are having difficulty filtering down enough material to reach the 30-second point, try this exercise: Take fifteen pieces of paper and write on each piece an item of information you would want to relay if you had all the time you wanted and could hold your party's attention level. Then remove the four least important, then another three, another two, and finally one more. The remaining five items probably will be the core of your oral resume.

Then organize your information into a clear, concise "30-second resume." Practice it aloud many times until you are comfortable repeating it and then try it with a friend for critique.

You may wish to end your oral resume with a "tickler," such as "What more would you like to know?" or "Is there something you would like for me to explain further?" This also has the advantage of beginning a dialogue and allows you to add information you may have wanted to include earlier.

In an informal or social setting, you also could ask, "Are you familiar with that industry?" or "Do you know someone who does that type of work?" If your listener does know someone, you are off to a fast start in your information gathering!

Just as you can vary your "tickler," you also may need to develop variations of your "30-second resume" to fit specific situations. For example, should you be talking with an authority in your industry, you could be more technical in your description than you would at a social gathering. In your "cold calling," you might wish to stress your ability to reduce costs or increase profits.

As your job search progresses, you undoubtedly will be surprised how often you will need this oral resume. Not only will it form the foundation of your networking campaign, but you also will use it on many other occasions. When you contact companies for the first time, when you attend network meetings, when you are asked the standard interview question, "Tell me about yourself" – these are only a few of the many times you will use your "30-second resume," so take the time to prepare it well.

Part 3

Business Cards

Why do you need business cards, even when you are unemployed?

There will be many occasions, especially in your networking efforts, when you will have the opportunity to discuss your job search with someone. Many of these meetings will be planned, but more often they will occur simply by chance. You want to leave your listener with contact data as well as a short summary of your expertise or job objective, and you cannot possibly carry copies of your resume at all times.

Oftentimes you will want to leave information with several persons, but when a full resume would be inappropriate. For example, when attending a professional association meeting, passing out your resume to many members would be viewed as obnoxious and criticized severely. Certainly you would not want to distribute your resume at a party or other social gathering. However, exchanging business cards is an accepted practice on nearly all occasions.

There are other, more practical reasons, too. Resumes cost more to print than business cards, and business cards are far easier to carry than an 8 1/2" x 11" pile of resumes. You can keep your business card in your pockets, wallet, purse, attaché case, car, or virtually anywhere. Furthermore, business cards are not only easier for you to handle, but your recipients are more likely to keep this small card than a bulky resume.

In order to give a longer lasting impression when exchanging your business card, a good practice is to personalize your card when possible. For example, write your nickname or most recent employer on the card when you hand it out.

In Appendix A, I have included some sample business cards. Note their simplicity, with only name, contact data, and employment objective, experience summary, or expertise. Do not attempt to condense your resume onto this small card, lest it look crowded and messy. As with your resume, do not design a flashy format or use colored paper. Again, this card is a reflection of you.

Business cards are inexpensive to have printed, as low as $10 for 1,000, depending on how much information you want to include.

Keep your business cards in an easily accessible place (*e.g.*, pocket or purse) and don't hesitate to give one out whenever you feel there is a possibility of developing a lead. Offering your business card will usually elicit a card in return, and you may wish to contact that person later.

CHAPTER IV

STEP THREE:

GET THAT INTERVIEW!

Part 1: The "Visible Market"

Part 2: Job Networking

Part 3: Useful Resources

CHAPTER IV

Step Three: Get That Interview!

Plan your attack!

I hesitate for this to sound like a battle plan, but maybe that is a good analogy. At any rate, this must be as well-planned and organized as any military assault. Get out the armaments – that is, the supplies I listed in Chapter II; you will need them now.

In our case, the military assault becomes a marketing assault. Every company develops a strategy for positioning its product or service in front of its buying public. Likewise, you will plan how to get yourself and/or your resume enough exposure to obtain interviews, the next step toward your new job.

The CAREER SEARCH SYSTEM includes thirteen marketing tools with which to develop your marketing plan. Depending on your background, you most likely will not need all thirteen, but if you do, the System is here to help. Each tool works best for certain types or levels of applicants, and I have indicated that information at the beginning of the discussion of each tool under *"Pro's"* and *"Con's."* In addition, each tool also has certain advantages and disadvantages, and those also are discussed.

Correctly utilized, these marketing tools will provide as many interviews as you can handle. You may even find yourself in the enviable position of having too many interviews! In that case, be careful not to tire yourself and interview poorly. Two interviews per day is all most individuals can handle successfully.

Before you begin your marketing assault, you must have your business cards and resumes prepared, especially your oral, "30-second resume." Chapter III detailed why you need these documents and how to prepare them, and examples of written resumes and business cards are included in Appendix A. All three are vital to the success of your efforts throughout the job hunt, so prepare them well.

Beginning your job search

There are essentially two approaches to conducting a job search, depending on which "job market" you utilize:

1) the "Visible Job Market"

2) the "Hidden Job Market"

The "Visible Job Market"

Career counselors generally agree that approximately 25% of all job vacancies fall into the first category, the "visible job market," which consists of those jobs that are
- advertised in classified want ads,
- recruited for by personnel agencies,
- available through job fairs,
- sought by corporate human resources departments, or
- available with federal, state, and local governments.

Locating these openings is the fastest and easiest course of action, and depending on your background, it may be all you will need to do. Individuals with experience in health care, computer science, or food service, for example, will find countless openings in their field through these sources. Applicants with between two and four years of career-related experience are always the most marketable, and they too may need only to tap into the "visible job market."

Nearly all job seekers will utilize these sources, and since they are easy and inexpensive, you too should use them. The CAREER SEARCH

SYSTEM describes fully how to obtain the best results from each source, and you need only follow the instructions.

The first six sources described in this chapter address the correct procedure you should follow in order to

- mass-mail your resume or background data to companies

- establish direct contact with companies, either through their personnel department or with a department manager,

- utilize personnel agencies and the services they offer,

- stand out from the crowd at job fairs,

- respond to classified want ads (Cover letters, salary histories, and other correspondences are discussed later in "Chapter VIII: Correspondence" and examples are given in Appendix B.), and

- apply for government positions.

The procedure for locating and applying for government openings is not as difficult as you may believe, and I even have found some shortcuts. Also, as the demand for government services increases in high-growth cities, the government payroll there also increases significantly.

Job Networking

In addition to this "visible job market," there are many other jobs available with companies, but as yet unadvertised and generally unknown, even within the company. There may be a planned addition, promotion, retirement, or replacement for which management has not yet begun a search. These plans may be only in the consideration stage now, awaiting further developments. In addition, companies often will create a new position if and when they find the "right" person.

These unpublicized openings are referred to as the **"Hidden Job Market,"** and experts generally agree that at least three-fourths of the jobs available at any time are part of this gray area. The primary way to locate them is through job networking, and Part 2 of this chapter details four methods to uncover them.

- Establishing a Job Network

- Attending networking clubs and meetings

- Networking through professional associations

- Using the "Information Interview"

Job networking is the most time-consuming and laborious method of job search, and to most job seekers, the most mysterious. Few job seekers understand the importance of job networking, and even those who do, have little knowledge of how or where to begin. *And yet more applicants find their job through some form of job networking than all other sources combined!*

The importance of job networking cannot be over-stressed. At least 70% (and I have read articles suggesting 85%) of all applicants will obtain new employment through this method, and thus you must incorporate it into your job search. The CAREER SEARCH SYSTEM leads you through it step-by-step, and you will be surprised how easily your networking progresses.

The sooner you begin developing your job network the sooner you will be employed!

Other useful resources

Part 3 of this chapter describes three more tools and how to use them in your search:

- Public agencies

- Privately funded organizations

- Useful publications

Charlotte is fortunate to have a number of free job search services, both public and privately funded, and I have detailed information regarding several. Most job seekers are not aware of these organizations and the extensive assistance they offer. Since they are free or inexpensive, you must incorporate them into your search.

I also have included a description of useful publications you may wish to add to your job search. Some of these will be helpful in locating companies to contact and others can be used in preparing for interviews. Most of these publications are free or low cost, or readily available at your local library.

Organizing your job search

If you have not yet organized according to the suggestions I outlined in Chapter II, you should do so now.

Next, plan your time. This is especially important if you are currently employed, since you will be limited in the amount of time you will have available for job search, and you must prioritize your efforts to maximize your results.[1]

If you are currently unemployed, how much time do you plan to spend job hunting? If your answer is other than at least 40 hours/week, think again! Perhaps being unemployed is an advantage here, since you will have enough time to conduct a thorough campaign. Continue to conduct your work-week as though you were still employed – which you are, only now your new job is finding a job.

Set up your notebook, using the forms illustrated on the next few pages, especially the weekly timetable form. Then read through all the sections on marketing tools and decide which ones you will use and in what time frame. Using your weekly timetable, schedule your time. This organization is more important than you may think, so don't shortcut.

You now are ready to begin your marketing assault! Read through every tool at least once, and then decide when and how you will use each one.

---

[1] For several reasons, companies prefer to hire individuals who are currently employed, and so I urge you not to resign your position in order to job hunt. Even if you are very unhappy with your job, I suggest you stick with it as long as possible, unless it becomes too difficult to conduct your job search effectively.

Sunday	Monday	Tuesday	Wednesday	Thursday	Friday	Saturday	Next week
Read Ads	Call Personnel Agencies	Personnel Agency Interview 8:30 A.M.	Research ABC Corp.	Practise interview w/ friend	OPEN — Catch-up!	Network w/ friends	ABC Corp interview Tuesday 10:00
Mail Ad Responses	Network w/ business Associates	Association meeting 6:30 p.m.					

Sample — Weekly Timetable

COMPANY "COLD CALLING"

Company (results)	Phone	Contact/title	Nothing	Sent + Resume
1. Matt. Mfg. Co.	847-1000	Katie Beam / Personnel	7/21	
2. Robts Co.	768-3400	Sam Rush / Treas.		7/22
3. Stephens & Collins Has opening! Call back 7/25.	471-1234	Sue Hummer / Acctg Mgr		7/22
4. ABC Corp Referred me to XYZ Supply Co.	231-9565	Bob Roe / Controller	7/21	
5.				
6.				
7.				
8.				
9.				
10.				

Sample direct contact form

PROFESSIONAL NETWORK CONTACTS

Name	Phone	Company	Title

(results)

1. Steve Reinking 568-7213 ABC Corp. Controller
Referred me to Linder Mfg. Co., whose controller
is Retiring.

2. Bill Johns 377-6430 Quik Corp Treasurer
Very friendly, may have leads, set up Info Interview for Tuesday

3. Susan Hope 761-3100 NC Financial Acctg Mgr
Very busy, no suggestions

4.

PERSONAL NETWORK CONTACTS

Name	Phone	Results

1. Bryan Smith 568-7213 Neighbor is VP
of H.R. w/ Mycorp. Will call + introduce me.

2. Joy Baer 721-3601 Her company is
expanding their Acctg staff. Will arrange i'view!

3. Harry Pitts 231-9556 No help now,
but will think about it.

4.

Networking forms

PART 1:

THE "VISIBLE JOB MARKET"

Tool #1: Mass Mailing

Tool #2: Direct Contact

Tool #3: Classified Advertising

Tool #4: Permanent Employment Agencies

Tool #5: Temporary Employment Agencies

Tool # 6: Job Fairs

Tool #7: Government Jobs

Tool #1: Mass-Mailing

Pro's: Contacts a large number of companies, easy to do, minimal expense, can be done during non-business hours.

Con's: Least effective job search method, time and labor intensive.

This is the oldest and simplest method of job search, and undoubtedly the most popular. It can be done at your convenience during evenings, weekends, or at any time you are not busy with other activities. Since it requires no face-to-face or verbal contact, it feels comfortable or at least non-threatening. Thus, this approach is tried by almost every job seeker.

The down side is that it is also the least productive method, probably securing fewer than 2% of all job offers. Nevertheless, since some applicants will find it successful and since you can plan it around your other job tools, you can use it also.

There are two approaches to this method:

     1) a selective mailing, in which you target companies more likely to have a need for your background, and

     2) a "resume blizzard," when you attempt to reach as many companies as possible.

Of course, your percentage of success will be much higher with the selective mailing, but that also may require time researching which companies you should contact. The other approach, obtaining a list of hundreds (maybe thousands!) of companies and blindly sending data to each one, generally results in an avalanche of rejection letters and very few promising leads.

Resume with cover letter vs. "broadcast letter"

Most mass mailings include a resume with cover letter. This cover letter mentions information not included in your resume (*e.g.*, why you have chosen to contact them, salary requirements, geographic restrictions, etc.) and emphasizes highlights in your background that will encourage the reader to peruse your resume. (See "Chapter VIII: Correspondence" for a full description and Appendix B for examples.)

An alternative method, the "broadcast letter," has gained popularity recently. Essentially, the broadcast letter is a one-page merger of the cover letter and the highlights of your resume. It tends to be more "reader friendly" by not including all of your experiences, but just the parts most likely to catch the reader's attention. It emphasizes accomplishments and achievements, and stresses what you can offer the company. Contact data is readily found and the reader is encouraged to call you for more information or an interview. Examples are included in "Appendix B: Correspondence."

The advantages to the broadcast letter are obvious. Since only one page is involved, it is simpler to handle and less expensive to mail. The primary disadvantage is of course that the reader has only limited information presented.

In speaking with applicants who have tried both methods, I have observed that for most mass-mailing, the broadcast letter is equally as successful as the resume with cover letter. Thus, I suggest that you use the broadcast letter with most of your mass-mailing, but use the resume/cover letter approach when you have reason to believe the company may have an opening for your experience.

Procedure

In planning to whom you will send your resume or other background information, imagine a series of concentric circles. At the center will be the companies most likely to be interested (*i.e.*, those that hire regularly in your field or for your discipline); the following ring will include companies you're not sure about but have reason to think might be interested; the next ring will be less certain; and the last ring will be the long shots.

• *Begin your mass-mailing with the center core* and expand outward as time permits. Determining which companies fall into each circle will require some research on your part, but the pay-off will be worth the effort. You probably already know many companies that will fall into the center, and the detailed company profiles I have included in Appendix C will provide more. Using the reference materials in the last section of this chapter will help you identify still more. After you have contacted those companies, you can spread into the outer rings.

• ***Keep accurate, well-organized records.*** As part of your overall organization, you should maintain a record of every company you contact and the results. You can make a list if you wish, but the simplest method is to keep a copy of your correspondence. This copy will include the date and the person you contacted, and you can write notes on the page regarding your activity there. Keep the pages in alphabetical order in a folder in your desk so that you can refer to it quickly when (not *if* – think positively!) a representative of the company calls. To help further with your organization, you may wish to separate the "core companies" correspondence from the others.

• ***To whom should you address your correspondence?*** Most job seekers will send it to the generic "personnel department," where it will be added to the pile of resumes already received. The more enterprising job seekers will send it to a specific department that will be more likely to need their background. But the job seekers who will be employed first will seek out the name or at least the title of the person responsible for hiring their experience.

However, if you don't know the name or title and don't have the time or ability to research the data, send your letter to "Human Resources." Later when you have more time or better information, you can re-contact the company, directing your information to a more appropriate source.

Conclusion

I have included this job search technique as Tool #1 because it is the most popular approach and the one most job seekers try first. That is unfortunate, since it really should be your last effort, to be used only after you have tried other more productive tools.

Why is a "resume blizzard" generally so unproductive? There are several reasons:

• I would be willing to wager any amount of money that at least 95% of the job seekers in Atlanta have sent their resume to Coca-Cola and BellSouth, two of the largest companies headquartered there. Likewise, in the Triad everyone contacts Wachovia, Burlington, and Sara Lee Corp.; and in the Triangle, IBM and Duke Power. Can you imagine the number of unsolicited resumes these large companies receive?

• Determining to whom you will direct your information is very difficult. There may be several persons within the company who sometimes seek your expertise, and you cannot hope to contact each of them. Human Resources should know of all job vacancies, but that is often not the case. And unless you indicate some person or department on your envelope, your resume could end up anywhere in the organization.

• Most of the new jobs being created in today's economy are not with major corporations. In fact, one reads daily about massive down-sizing and lay-offs at the Fortune 500-type corporations. The growing job markets are in small- to medium-size companies, generally not included on any list of companies you may locate.

Mass mailings work best for only certain types of job applicants, generally those with highly desirable experience. Otherwise, the more years of experience you have, the more frustrating you will find this method.

Nevertheless, if you have the time and inclination, I suggest that you go ahead and send your resume to companies in which you have a strong interest or feel that they often may have needs for your background. Most of all, it will make you feel good that you are doing something constructive toward your job search, and there is a definite possibility you might uncover an opportunity, either for an interview now or for a networking source later. However, be prepared for the downside – the rejection letters – and don't slip into depression because of them.

And relax. The CAREER SEARCH SYSTEM describes twelve other sources. If this one is not the right one for you, several of the others will be.

Tool #2: Direct Contact

Pro's: Works best for entry- and mid-level positions, especially for applicants with less than six or seven years of experience. Ideally suited for recent grads, first job changers, and persons seeking a specific industry or company. Good approach for individuals with experience and knowledge in one industry.

Con's: Labor intensive, especially in locating hiring authorities. Less effective for applicants with extensive experience that is not in one industry.

There are two reasons for directly contacting a company without prior knowledge of their current job needs:

1) They may have a job opening for your background, and you can arrange an interview with them.

2) You can obtain some useful information and/or job leads.

This section discusses the first reason; the second reason is discussed in Part 2 of this chapter on Job Networking.

Most importantly, don't waste your time and money by blindly contacting companies that you know little about. That "shotgun" approach generally is not effective, in time, cost, or results. There are other sources to those companies, such as personnel agencies, newspaper ads, networking, etc. Use your time wisely, and concentrate your direct contact efforts on the companies that regularly hire for your specialty or an industry that can use your specific experience. Unlike other books that are hardly more useful than the Yellow Pages, the CAREER SEARCH SYSTEM has researched the hiring practices of hundreds of companies. The result of this research is a selected list of companies (Appendix C) that omits companies that seldom have personnel needs, in favor of targeting firms that do the most professional-level hiring – which incidentally, are not necessarily the companies with the largest numbers of employees.

From my personal experiences and through research, I have compiled a list of the most active employers in the Triangle and Triad area, found in Appendix C. These companies were selected for diversity and for the number of applicants hired each year. I have tried to include examples from as many industries and professions as possible, and you probably will be interested in many. My associates or I spoke with each of these companies personally, and thus, the information is current and accurate, according to their staffing specialists.

Mounting a Direct Contact Campaign

Scan through the list of companies in Appendix C and then using a highlighting marking pen, mark those in which you have an interest and those that hire in your specialty. I have included a thorough description of their operations and hiring procedures, as well as the types of applicants frequently sought and whether the company seeks entry-level and/or experienced personnel. Read through the company profiles and you will find practically any and every job description included many times.

Next, add several pages in your notebook to record your efforts. Use the sample form "Company Cold Calling," or one similar, and list the companies you plan to contact. (When you call, be sure to include the date, as I illustrated.) In addition to the large corporations detailed in Appendix C, you may know of other companies who hire in your field or for your specialty and that you wish to contact.

Be selective and don't make your list too long, since making a personal contact is time consuming. Long shots generally are not productive and definitely will expend time you otherwise might use more productively. Choose companies that you have reason to think may have openings in your field or that may be expanding their general work force.

Whom should I contact?

This is a debatable question, with many career counselors giving one answer and personnel managers another. As with most debates, there are good reasons to support both sides.

Most, if not all, career counselors would suggest that you should make your initial company contact with a "hiring authority," that is, a department manager who has control over the personnel requirements in a specific department. One reason is that this person may have current or projected personnel needs that have not been requisitioned from Human Resources[1] or Personnel Recruiting. Secondly, this manager will most likely be the ultimate decision-maker with whom you would eventually interview, and thus you are a step ahead by starting here. This logic concludes that Personnel Departments are often another hurdle and should be by-passed when possible.

There are many reasons why Personnel Departments may not be aware of all the needs within their companies. A manager often will have plans to add to or alter the department in the future and may consider going ahead with the change now, if your background fits the need. Also, some department heads prefer to hire direct, rather than using their recruiting staff, who may be busy with other assignments. Furthermore, some companies are very decentralized and encourage managers to conduct their own personnel search and hiring. There are many other reasons, too, more than we can discuss here.

Most personnel managers would disagree with those assumptions, and strongly feel that you should contact them first. It is their function within the company to interview and screen applicants, following federal and local statutes, as well as company policies and procedures; these guidelines may be unknown to executives attempting to conduct their own hiring. These personnel professionals have been trained to interview carefully and thoroughly, and they should be more in tune to the overall needs of the company, not just one department.

In addition, some department managers may find your contact a nuisance, and you will be off to a bad start. Personnel may feel you are trying to short-circuit them, and they too will be annoyed. And finally, some companies have a firm policy that all initial contacts with applicants must be through Personnel.

But perhaps the best reason for contacting Personnel is simply expedience. Large companies will have many department managers over your specialty, and you cannot expect to contact all of them. Also, you may not have the time or resources to trace all the hiring authorities

---

[1]Although the vogue designation for the old, generic term "Personnel Department" is now "Human Resources," not all companies use that name. In addition, larger companies will also have a separate Recruiting or Staffing specialty within Human Resources. Although there can be definite distinctions, I have used these terms fairly interchangeably, and for our purposes here, that is adequate.

within a company. In these cases, you must utilize the company's Personnel Department.

Although in my practice I generally work with Personnel, I adhere more to the former reasoning. I understand Personnel's concerns, but tend to agree that it is better to contact a hiring authority, especially when you have a friend or contact within the company who can tell you whom to contact. (Of course, this person may also tell you that the company requires you to start with Personnel.) However, you can assuage Personnel by also sending them a resume, noting whom you have already contacted.

"Cold Calling"

Now comes the laborious part: "cold calling" each company. In your "cold calling" section, list the companies you plan to contact, using a form similar to the one illustrated earlier in this chapter. Ideally, you should speak by phone personally with an official at each company, but that is not always possible. The company representative may not be available, or you may not have the time or facility, especially if you are currently employed. In these cases, you should mail a resume and include a cover letter. (The cover letter is explained in Chapter VIII.)

Many people have a fear of the phone, and if you are one of them, you need to overcome your apprehensions. Preparing and rehearsing what you plan to say on the phone will help, as well as having your "30-Second Resume" prepared and ready to use. I mentioned earlier that you would be using this oral resume often, and now is one of those times. If you missed the discussion of this topic, it was described in Part 2 of "Chapter III: Preparing Your Resumes."

Procedure to follow

Regardless of whether you contact Personnel or a department manager, the procedure is the same. In Appendix C I have listed most of Charlotte's largest hiring companies, and the procedure to follow if you go through Personnel. Note that in the company list, I have indicated the Personnel contact by job title or department, not by name. This is because the interviewing authority frequently changes and you will lose valuable time trying to contact or sending a resume to the wrong person. It is useful, however, to know the name of the interviewing authority, and that is one of the purposes in calling the companies directly.

When the company receptionist answers your call, ask for the Whomever (the department or job title I indicated as the contact, or the department manager you are seeking). When Whomever's secretary answers, say, "Hello. My name is Whatever, and I am seeking a position in _____(or as a _____). May I speak with Whomever?" Most likely at this point, you will be instructed to send your resume, in which case ask for the name of the person to whom you should address it, and record the name in your notebook. Don't be upset, however, if you are not given the name; some companies have a policy forbidding the disclosure of employee names.

If you actually do get the opportunity to speak with Whomever, you must be prepared. This is your chance to make a positive impression, have a brief telephone interview, and schedule a personal interview also. Fortunately, you are a tempo ahead, because you already have composed and rehearsed a brief summary of your qualifications – the "30-second resume"! You may have only one shot here, so make it count.

If it appears that they do have an interest or need for your background, offer to come for a personal interview, if this is possible for you. If you are talking with the company's interviewer, you must be ready for this telephone interview. Prepare and practice your interviewing techniques in advance, and don't be caught by surprise. (See "Chapter V: Interviewing Techniques.")

If your contact states that there are no job opportunities available there, try to turn the call into a networking or information call. Ask for suggestions in your job search. Is he/she aware of openings with other companies for your background? Even better, would he/she consider spending a few minutes with you in an "information interview." This "information interview" is discussed later in the chapter as "Tool #9" and you should have read that section before beginning your "cold calling." (Actually, you should read this entire book at least once before beginning any part of your job search!)

Assuming you were instructed to mail your resume, you will also need to include a cover letter. Having already written your resume, writing this will be easy. Chapter VIII is a thorough discussion of correspondence, especially cover letters and their different purposes and forms. Several examples are included in Appendix B.

In the closing paragraph of your cover letter, you will have said that you plan to telephone them in a few days. Definitely do so. You want to know if your resume was received or lost along the way, and if it has been reviewed. Does the company have an opening for someone with your credentials? Is it being routed to another department or department manager? Are there any questions they would like to ask or additional information they need? As always, record the results of your phone call in your notebook.

Finally, you will recall that I suggested you contact department managers whenever possible; but this is not to say that you should ignore Human Resources or Recruiting. In fact, if you are told by the department manager that no opening currently exists, I suggest you also contact Personnel. Individual departments and their managers seldom keep a resume file, but Human Resources usually will, and another need for your background may arise later.

Even if the department manager does request your resume, you may wish to send one to Personnel as well, especially if you do not hear back from this manager within a reasonable time period. This is because the manager may be too busy with other projects to consider you now, but there may be another opening somewhere else within the company. Also, just as the Personnel Department may not be aware of projected needs within other departments, those department managers may not be aware of upper management's plans.

In summary, don't look upon personnel departments as just another hurdle to be avoided whenever possible, but rather utilize them when necessary or expedient. They have a purpose within their companies, and you should make use of it.

Telephone Etiquette

In today's high-tech world, on many of your phone calls, you may be connected with your party's answering machine, "voice mail," or some other verbal device, and you will be asked to leave your name, phone number, and "a brief message." I nearly always do leave a message and have been pleasantly surprised at the high rate of times I have had my call returned.

I too have an answering machine, to cover the times when I am out of my office or otherwise unavailable to receive calls. My pet peeve has become the callers who leave an incoherent or inaudible message, and I am forced to replay the message several times. For example,

• they speak so rapidly that I cannot understand, especially in relaying their phone number;

• they have an unusual name or a foreign name that is difficult to understand or spell;

• their message is garbled or their thoughts are unorganized.

On those occasions when you are referred to an answering service, I suggest you do leave a message, but with the knowledge that a poor message will have created a poor impression, and that may result in your call not being returned. Speak your name and phone number clearly, leave your prepared message (short and well-enunciated), then repeat your name and phone number. End your message with "Thank you and I look forward to speaking with you soon." Unless your name is a very common name like Smith or Jones, you should spell it. Most importantly, say your phone number slowly and clearly.

Conclusion

The **CAREER SEARCH SYSTEM** outlines many different and effective sources for obtaining interviews and job offers, and not all of them will apply to you. Quite frankly, the direct contact source has limited success unless you fit one of these categories:

1) You have extensive experience within one industry or discipline, and that experience would be useful to most companies within that industry or discipline.

2) You have less than five years experience and can still be cross-trained into other functions within your discipline.

3) You have highly desirable experience or academic background. For example, most medical specialties, restaurant managers or computer science professionals are very much in demand and have no difficulty in finding employment with any number of companies.

If you do not fit into one of those descriptions, the direct contact source is not the one where you should be concentrating your efforts. That is my major complaint with books that list hundreds (thousands?)

of companies, and suggest that you call, contact, or send your resume to as many as possible. There are other sources in the **CAREER SEARCH SYSTEM** that will benefit you more.

Tool #3: Classified Advertisements

Pro's: Cheap and easy source of many listings, covering all disciplines and levels. Good place to start. Good source to locate personnel agencies, as well as companies not using agencies, and small companies with infrequent needs. Often quotes salary. Local companies can be quick interviews.

Con's: You can get lost in the crowd of responses. May be difficult to discern good opportunities.

The largest source of announced openings in the Triangle and Triad is contained in the classified ads section of the Sunday edition of the major local newspapers. These are a "must" in your search.

The largest classified section is in the Raleigh newspaper,*The News & Observer;* to order a subscription call (919) 829-4700 or (800) 522-4205 and charge your subscription to MasterCard or Visa. Greensboro's *News & Record* is also sizable; order by calling (800) 553-6880.

These classified sections are by far the largest in the region. Within the twenty or so pages of ads will be up to 5,000 job openings, advertised by both companies and personnel agencies. These openings are listed alphabetically by numerous job categories (accounting/financial, data processing, engineers, sales, etc.). Peruse the categories that apply to you, and circle in red the openings for which you plan to apply.

In addition to locating current job openings, perusing these ads can yield other information. You can determine which disciplines and industries are growing, because these will be mentioned most often. Conversely, shrinking job categories will be conspicuous by their absence. If you are contemplating a career change or undecided on which career to pursue (as so many recent college grads are), reviewing these ads can help you decide. Further, if there is a retailer near you who sells many newspapers from across the country, you can compare the size of the want ads from several cities to get an idea of the job prospects in each city.

In choosing which ads to consider, keep in mind that if the ad sounds too good to be true, it probably is. Newspapers try to screen their clients, but bogus or misleading ads sometimes slip by. Here is one clue: if you call a company, and someone answers with the phone number and then refuses to reveal the company's name, hang up!

Although *The News & Observer* and *The News & Record* are the largest source of classified ads covering the Triangle and Triad areas, there are other local papers that also have Sunday editions with classified ads.

- *The Herald Sun* covers Durham, (919) 419-6900

- *Winston-Salem Journal*, (910) 727-7456

In addition, the Sunday classified ads in *The Atlanta Journal-Constitution* frequently will include openings for cities throughout the Southeast. To subscribe, call (800) 282-1493, extension 5024. You will be billed or you can charge to a credit card.

Another excellent source of classified ads is professional and trade magazines. If you have access to any periodicals in your field, review them and answer any classified ads that seem fruitful; these ads are usually on the last few pages of the publication. Respond to them as you would a newspaper ad. This source is especially helpful in determining which personnel agencies specialize in your field, since they are the ones that would place advertisements in specific journals.

Procedure

Peruse the job categories that apply to you and circle in red the openings, both company and personnel agency, for which you plan to apply. After you have finished scrutinizing the ads, cut out the company (not agency) ads you circled and tape them onto blank pages to put in your notebook, in the section you labeled "Classified Ads." Leave lots of empty space beside the ads, to record your activity with them, including dates contacted and results.

Now, cut out the personnel agency ads. You may notice that one agency is advertising several jobs for which you will want to apply.

Write the name of each agency at the top of a page and then tape the corresponding ads to the page, and include it in your "Personnel Agencies" section. Leave space on the page to record activity with that agency.

Now go back to the company ads and contact each one. If the company included its phone number or did not specifically forbid phone calls, I suggest you call them and ask if you can speak with someone regarding the opening. If you do get through to the recruiter, you must be prepared for an interview then, so before calling, you should study "Chapter V: Interviewing Techniques." Also, here is another opportunity to use your "30-second resume"!

Most likely, however, you will be instructed to mail your resume before you speak with anyone personally regarding the position. Politely ask to whom you should address the resume, and record the information in your notebook. Including that person's name on your envelop and cover letter is an optional but personal touch, and some recruiters will note it. Don't be surprised, however, if the receptionist has been instructed not to give out that information.

Along with your resume, you will include a cover letter. Refer to Chapter VIII for a description and to Appendix B for illustrations. In your notebook, record the date you sent your resume, when you called to follow-up, and the results.

Responding to personnel agency advertisements will be slightly different, and after reading the next two sections on personnel agencies, you will better understand the distinctions. Whenever possible, call them before sending a resume. By talking with them first, you can ascertain if you fit their available openings and whether or not that particular agency will be able to help you. Operating procedures vary from agency to agency, some requiring that you send a resume first, others requesting you to come in for a personal interview and bring your resume. If you are instructed to mail your resume, ask to whom you should address it and record that name in your notebook on the page for that agency. Some agencies will have several persons handling the same opening, and so there may not be a specific contact person.

A formal cover letter is not necessary to send to agencies, although you may if that is convenient. Just a short typed or handwritten note with your salary requirements and restrictions (if any) is sufficient. Keep in mind, however, that this note is the agency's first impression of you and you must impress them in order to be referred to their client. Additional information on the use of this interview source is contained in the next section of this chapter.

"Blind Ads"

Oftentimes companies advertise their job vacancies without identifying themselves, and you are instructed to mail your resume to a post office box number. These are called "blind ads," since they do not reveal the name of the employer. You may be interested in the openings but hesitant to reveal your name and information without knowing whom you are contacting. I have heard of individuals who responded to a blind ad, only to learn that the ad was submitted by their own company! Unfortunately, their employment was terminated as a result.

If the company is using their own post office box, you can obtain the company name before sending your resume by calling the post office branch that handles the zip code in the address listed. Ask who rents that specific box number, and if the box is rented to a company or someone who conducts business through that mail box, the post office will give you the name.

Conclusion

If you have mailed your resume to a company, plan to call them in a few days to confirm that your resume was received. Ask if there are questions or additional information needed to complete your application. And, of course, offer to come for an interview at their convenience.

Just as you would prepare for a face-to-face interview, be ready for a phone screening also. Telephone interviews are usually short and cover only basic information. Typical questions will revolve around why you are seeking new employment and if you have the background needed for the job. If you pass this quick test, you will be invited for an interview.

Here's a final word on classified ads, and this applies to direct contact and personnel agencies as well. A personal, face-to-face interview is always preferable to indirect contact, regardless of how good your resume looks. Thus, whenever possible, try to be seen, rather than just heard. If you are very interested in a specific position and have been able to speak with a company interviewer on the phone, press for an interview time or at least offer to bring by your resume in person. And if you do deliver your resume in person, ask to simply meet the interviewer, if he/she is available.

Tool #4: Permanent Employment Agencies

Pro's: Probably the largest source of job openings. Easy and convenient. Good agencies will supply you not only with interviews, but also information on the company, the job, and the interviewer. Can work well at all levels and fields. Usually free. Good source for quick interviews.

Con's: Not usually successful for hard-to-place applicants. Not easy to find most useful agencies. Fee sometimes involved, especially at lower-level openings.

The number of job openings represented collectively by the various personnel agencies in the Triangle and Triad can be numbered in the tens of thousands. There are literally hundreds of these agencies here, filling many pages in the Yellow Pages and in at least three different listing categories. Because they represent so many companies and opportunities, they should be an invaluable source for you.

Oftentimes, this industry receives a lot of bad press, much of it deservedly so. Some of these firms are excellent and do a very creditable job, and thus they are highly regarded and utilized by their client companies. But unfortunately, some agencies are downright awful. How do you select one?

First of all, don't select one; select several. Every agency would like to have you as its exclusive applicant, but "putting all your eggs in one basket" is not in your best interest. Rather, make yourself available to whichever ones can offer you exposure to the best companies and positions.

Understand, too, that every agency specializes in a certain level (entry, middle management, executive, etc.) or areas (clerical, management, engineering, etc.), and there are probably personnel agencies or individuals within an agency that specialize in your field. Your task is to zero in on the ones that handle applicants at your level and in your field of specialty, without trying to call every personnel agency listed in the phone book.

Selecting your agencies

The North Carolina Association of Personnel Services publishes a directory of their membership, including the specialties of each member. Most of their local information is included in Appendix D. In addition, there are excellent agencies who are not members, and thus I suggest you use the procedure listed below.

- _Call corporate human resources departments._ The best method for locating older, more established agencies is to call the personnel department (or a specific department manager) of a few major Atlanta companies and ask which permanent employment firms they use for your discipline and if they would recommend a specific recruiter there. This has the advantage of not only finding an agency, but also talking with a corporate personnel professional who may have other suggestions as well. In addition, when you then call the agencies that were recommended, be certain to mention the company and/or the individual who recommended them, and I guarantee you will get a warm reception!

- _Read the classified ads._ You also should contact newer agencies, since they often are more aggressive and may give you more attention. These agencies probably will advertise in the Sunday classified section of the local newspapers. Pick out the agencies that are advertising for positions that interest you and contact two or three.

- _Network.._ Ask friends and business associates which agencies they have used and would recommend. When attending job networking or professional association meetings, ask several people if they have used an agency or recommend one. This is especially helpful if the person you ask has a background similar to your own.

- _Check with college career placement departments_ If you graduated from a local college, check with the Career Placement Department and ask for recommendations. In addition, you can call a university's academic department that covers your background, and ask if they are aware of agencies that specialize in your field.

- _Review theTelephone Yellow Pages._ Although you should not waste your time calling every agency in the phone book, nevertheless you should peruse the Yellow Pages under the headings "Employment Agencies" and "Executive Search Consultants" to see if there are agencies who specialize in your field. Oftentimes these agencies will have your industry as part of their name (*e.g.*, "Restaurant Recruiters" or "Insurance Personnel Search") or they may have a box ad that mentions your specialty.

• *Locate specialized periodicals.* Still another excellent source is the back pages of trade newspapers and magazines. Agencies who advertise in these specialized journals usually concentrate on that discipline in their recruiting.

Lastly, to inquire if there are complaints about any agencies in general or specifically about the one(s) you are considering, call the local Better Business Bureau.
   • Raleigh-Durham: Better Business Bureau of Eastern NC, (919) 872-9240
   • Greensboro: Better Business Bureau of Central NC, (910) 862-4240
   • Winston-Salem: Better Business Bureau, (910) 725-8348

Contacting your agencies

Once you have selected the agencies that you plan to use, here is the procedure to follow. Whenever possible, you should visit them personally for two reasons:

1) to determine if they can adequately represent you or if you want them to represent you, and

2) to make a personal impression on them, so they can better present you to their clients.

If you are not local, call them to ask if they can help you. If you are instructed to send in a resume, do so, and then call back in a few days to check on the activity in your behalf. Ask them frankly if they will be able to arrange interviews and in what time frame. Be polite, but persistent. Can they help you or are you wasting your time? When would they like for you to call again? Do they have any suggestions for you? Since they have reviewed your resume, ask for their opinion of it.

Types of Personnel Agencies

Understanding the nature of personnel agencies and how they work will enable you to better utilize their services. Most importantly, realize that they are not philanthropic organizations; they are in business to make a profit. Their income is derived entirely from fees collected through their efforts at matching applicants with client companies.

Agencies can be broadly categorized into three groups, related to the sources of their income:

- Executive search firms

- Temporary agencies

- Contingency agencies

Executive search firms, sometimes called "headhunters," are retained by companies to search for specific personnel needs and are paid in advance by the retaining company. Since they work on a limited number of specific cases, they generally are not a good source for entry- and mid-level positions. Senior-level executives, however, may benefit from search firms that specialize in their area of expertise.

Temporary agencies derive their income from providing companies with contract labor, for which the company pays the agency and the agency in turn pays the laborers. The use of temporary agencies has increased tremendously in the past few years, and these firms offer some excellent opportunities to secure permanent employment. A detailed discussion explaining how to use these agencies is included in the next section as Tool #5.

By far the largest number of agencies falls into the third group, called **contingency agencies**, and these will be your best source to call. These firms are paid only when one of their applicants accepts employment through their efforts with one of their client companies, and thus, their fee is contingent upon making the placement. These agencies will have many job openings in many diverse industries and with many different companies, and some of these companies also may have listed the same opening with other agencies.

Remember that since they are paid only when they make a job placement, they are most interested in applicants who fit the current needs of their clients, and if you are more difficult to place than another applicant, you will not get as much attention. When talking with them, state your employment objective, but be as flexible as possible and listen to their suggestions. However, you are under no obligation to accept any interview that does not meet your standards.

Interview with the agency as though it is the company with whom you hope to be employed. Many companies have established a strong rapport with the agency(s) they use and have great confidence in the agency's opinion. Thus, you must impress the agency enough to be referred on to these key clients.

At the end of your interview, ask how soon you can expect to hear from them and when you will be sent on an interview. Also, seek their frank appraisal of your resume and interviewing skills, and ask if they have any suggestions or recommendations for you to consider.

During this interview, you should ask questions that will help you to evaluate the agency, the agency interviewer, and the assistance they can offer you. Personnel agencies have notoriously high employee turnover, and your interviewer may have been at the job for only a very short while. If this is the case, an opinion of your resume and interviewing skills may be totally useless. In addition, this trainee may not understand your background and experience, and will not be able to present you to potential clients.

Working with Agencies

You have every reason to expect the agencies you select to treat you honestly and fairly. They should never send you on interviews for which you are not qualified[1] or refer you to positions in which you have no interest. You should be briefed before each interview regarding the nature of the position, promotional potential, salary range, and company background. The best agencies will maintain files in their office of company literature for you to peruse, including annual reports and recruiting information, especially for their best clients. Many agencies also know their client's interviewers and interviewing techniques.

---

[1] Over the years, I have had many candidates insist that if I would just set the interview for them, they would "sell themselves" enough to get the job, regardless of their lack of qualifications. I never would waste their time or my clients' time in such a fruitless arrangement, and they often could not understand why. Believe me, an agency that somehow finagles an interview for you for which you are not at all qualified is not doing you any favors. They are wasting your time and their (soon-to-be-former) clients' patience.

In return, you should treat your agencies with the same respect you expect from them. If you are not interested in a specific interview, tell the agency why; this will help your recruiter to be more selective for future interviews. Always show up for your interviews or advise the agency well in advance to cancel; most agencies will not work with you once you have failed to show for an scheduled interview. Call your agency recruiter immediately after each interview to relay your impressions of the interview.

Your personnel agencies' recruiters can become good, professional friends, and you should treat them as you would other professionals. I still talk with applicants I placed more than twenty years ago!

Agency Contracts and Fees

If the agency requires you to sign a contract, read it carefully before you sign and be sure to get a copy. Agency contracts are fairly standard, and generally speaking, you need not worry about signing one. The important facts to know are these:

1) You do not have to accept any offer extended. Do not allow the agency to pressure you into accepting a position you do not want.

2) No fee is involved until you do accept employment as a result of their service.[1]

However, before you accept a position through a personnel agency, be certain you understand your legal liability, if any, to the agency. For example, are there any circumstances under which you may be held responsible for all or part of the fee? Are you required to remain with the company for a period of time before your liability to the agency expires? If the company defaults on the fee, are you obligated for it? If you are uncomfortable with any part of the contract, get a written waiver from the agency before you accept the position.

---

[1] There is one extenuating circumstance of which you should be aware. In the past, I have seen agency contracts that required a portion of your salary increase, should you accept a counter-offer from your present company. The basis for this is that your increase is a direct result of their efforts in obtaining you other employment, which then forced your present company to make you the counter-offer. Thus, before accepting a counter-offer, confirm that you are under no contractual obligation to the agency or that your present company will pay the fee.

When I first began agency recruiting twenty years ago, most personnel agencies accepted job openings that were both "fee paid" (*i.e.*, the hiring company pays the agency fee) and "non-fee paid" (*i.e.*, the applicant pays the fee). Salaries were lower then and since the agency's fee is based on a percentage of their placement's first-year's income, consequently so were agency fees. In addition, the concept of companies paying an agency fee was not so well accepted.

Times have changed, and the reverse is currently true. Most professional-level personnel agencies now handle only positions in which the hiring company pays the agency's fee, and these "fee paid" positions cost you nothing. I strongly recommend that you restrict your initial agency contacts to those handling only "fee paid" openings, and if necessary, you can call the other agencies later.

However, if you have limited qualifications (and this often happens to trainees), you may find yourself in the uncomfortable position of considering a job offer that requires you to pay a fee. I personally have a strong disdain for companies that will not pay an agency fee and yet willingly hire through personnel agencies, knowing that the high expense of the agency fee will be passed on to their new employee. Nevertheless, if you find yourself in this situation, be absolutely, 100% certain you want that job before you saddle yourself with the large financial burden of an agency fee. Try to negotiate with the agency for a lesser amount or with the company for a reimbursement later. Better still, stay away from this situation to begin with.

Agency Scams

There is one more situation you unfortunately may encounter: the "up-front fee" agency or some other business that requires you to pay a fee in advance of any job assistance. This fee may be only $75 or $100 for a list of job openings (usually copied from the newspaper), or they can soar up to several thousand dollars for "counseling" or resume distribution. Outlawed in many states, some of these scams will pose as personnel agencies and sell you lists of alleged job openings, guarantee you employment after their fee is paid, or some other useless "service."

Just this morning I read of an FBI sting on a business operating in Atlanta and Chicago that guaranteed overseas employment for a fee of $295, but in fact had no jobs to offer and kept the money. Beware of these crooks and before you hand over your money, ask for references or call the Better Business Bureau.[1]

Summary

Personnel agencies, both permanent and temporary, can be an excellent source and you should use them when possible, but recognize they do have limitations. If you are seeking employment in a very narrow field (*e.g.*, public relations or staff marketing), they likely will be of little help. If there is something in your background that makes you less marketable than their other applicants, you will not have good results with them. As I stated before, the best approach with agencies is to ask for a frank analysis of the help they can offer you.

I frequently speak with applicants who have been offended by a personnel agency – not that they were really mistreated, but rather they were made to feel like one of the herd, impersonal and dehumanized. Instead of "good-bye," they wanted to say "moo" or "baa." Perhaps their interview was cold, short, and perfunctory, or frequently interrupted. Another major complaint I often hear is that phone calls were not returned promptly, or even at all.

I won't make excuses for this behavior on the part of agencies, but I will explain why it happens, and I even will admit some guilt myself. Remember back to the resume chapter when I stated that I often receive up to 100 or so responses per advertisement. Then you must understand that each personnel agent will be handling many, many applicants at all times. Unfortunately, we often do not have enough time to appease everyone and still do our work.

So don't let yourself be offended to the point of cutting yourself off from any possible source of leads and interviews. Your purpose is to use the agencies for your benefit, and don't lose sight of that objective, regardless of how you may feel toward the agency. I assure you that they mean no personal affront.

However, should you have a complaint regarding the ethics of a specific agency, you may seek redress through the North Carolina

---

[1] I must make a distinction between these shams and legitimate "outplacement" firms. Those latter firms can be very helpful and are often part of a severance package offered by employers. If you have doubts as to a firm's legitimacy, check their references.

Association of Personnel Services. Their members supposedly adhere to a code of ethics and you can register your complaint by calling their office at (910) 545-1887, or writing to

Becca McLeod, Executive Director
NCAPS
P O Box 4174, Greensboro, NC 27404.

And remember, this source is only one of the many you have available. Don't make the mistake of waiting for an agency to find you a job when you have other sources to tap.

Tool #5: Temporary Employment Agencies

Pro's: Quick source of income, offers possibility of permanent job, good networking source, variety of companies and assignments, maintains skills.

Con's: Often low salary, difficult to explore other companies while employed, not permanent, limited benefits, no promotional opportunity.

Companies sometimes need additional help, but for many reasons are reluctant to take on new, permanent employees. An increasingly popular solution to this dilemma is to hire temporary employees, utilizing the services of a temporary employment agency.

Temporary agencies derive their income from providing companies with contract labor, for which the company pays the agency and the agency in turn pays the laborers. Most often this is for hourly or clerical work, but some firms offer long-term contracts, especially for engineers and other specialized work. There are also temporary agencies specializing in short-term professional-level openings, most often in accounting and data processing.

In the past few years, many more companies have discovered the advantages of hiring temporaries. Labor costs are cut, since the company does not pay benefits or payroll taxes and does not need to maintain personnel records. "Temps," as they are euphemistically termed, are hired only for as long as needed or to fill a short-term replacement. There usually is no interviewing process and temps are available almost instantly.

Some individuals maintain a career working temp. They cite the variety of jobs and companies, the freedom to work when they want, and the knowledge gained from working different assignments as the advantages of this career path. However, for our discussion we will consider temporary employment only as a stepping stone to permanent positions.

In a recent report aired on National Public Radio, the reporter stated that of the total new jobs created in the past year, one in five was for a temporary employee. Extrapolating that national statistic for the Atlanta area, more than 16,000 new temporary jobs have been created here this year. Moreover, in my recent survey of Atlanta's largest employers, 90+% indicated they regularly employ temps.

Working a temporary assignment offers you three new options for finding other employment:

(1) The position may be "temp-to-perm."

(2) While on the assignment, you can job network through other company employees, vendors, or clients.

(3) Once inside the company, you can review the company's in-house job postings and apply for other employment there.

"Temp-to-perm"

"Temp-to-perm" positions are jobs that are classified by the company as temporary, but may become permanent within a short period. These positions may be for any discipline, including clerical, accounting, engineering, data processing, marketing, etc., and can be for short- or long-term assignments. When applying through a temporary agency, always ask what they have available in "temp-to-perm."

Oftentimes, a company will want to test an employee before committing to a definite job. For example, I am aware of a major Atlanta corporation that regularly hires several temps for customer service positions. After a few months, those temps who have performed their tasks well are offered permanent employment. Those temps who have difficulty with the assignments are not retained.

Another example is a growing company that needs additional help but is not ready to hire a new employee. A temp can fill the current urgency, and if the expansion continues, the position can become permanent.

Networking

Since you were hired as a temporary employee, the company should have no objection to tactful efforts at job networking. Comparing job search techniques and information with other temps can be a useful exchange of ideas. Permanent employees may be aware of vacancies within their company or openings they learned about through clients. You also may be able to discuss your job search with vendors or clients, but be discreet.

For example, I know of an accountant whose supervisor on a temporary assignment referred him to the company's CPA firm for placement. Also, we recently hired a temporary receptionist who was seeking a sales position in the hospitality industry; I know the personnel manager with a major hotel here and referred her to them. As with all job networking, the possibilities are infinite.

Remember, however, that you have been employed to perform a specific task. Do not allow your job networking efforts to interfere with your assigned duties.

In-house job postings

One of the advantages of working temp, especially at a large company, is that you will be privy to the company's "in-house job postings," i.e., listings of jobs currently available with the company, including functional descriptions and basic requirements. You can peruse the information and then apply for positions for which you qualify.

Every corporation strives to fill new job vacancies with current employees whenever possible, especially promotions. Promoting from within is good for company morale, and there are financial and practical advantages as well. But the best reason for promoting current employees is that the employee's work performance has been carefully observed by supervisors, who are in a position to offer critical comments and recommendations.

As a temporary employee, you also will report to a supervisor, who will be familiar with the quality of your work and who will be called upon for a recommendation (or rejection!) of your application for permanent employment. A good report from your supervisor will weigh heavily in the decision to hire you.

Thus, approach each temporary job as if it were a pre-employment test or part of the interviewing process. Even if the position for which you are applying has nothing to do with your temporary assignment, the quality of your work and the attitude you demonstrate can determine whether or not you are offered the job. Further, if you feel certain that your supervisor is pleased with your work, consider asking him/her to intercede in your behalf.

Other advantages

Another reason for working temp is the opportunity to learn new skills, or maintain and improve existing skills. For example, if your background is in data processing, working a temp position in your field might expose you to new software or new applications for procedures you already knew. At the very least, you would preserve your current level of competency.

Many temporary agencies offer training classes in the new, "hot" fields, especially in data processing. These classes are free and you can include the added knowledge on your resume.

In the past few years, many large corporations have established in-house temporary services that staff positions primarily for their firm. Nearly all of these positions offer a route to permanent, full-time employment with that company, either through "temp-to-perm" or company job postings. If you have determined a specific company best fits your objectives, working through their temp agency affords an excellent opportunity to start a career there.

Conclusion

As you see, working temp offers many advantages. It provides you with income, skill and knowledge development, networking potential, and the possibility of permanent employment. Best of all, you can continue your job search in your time off, showing that you are currently employed.

One major downside, however, is that you will lose your unemployment benefits while working temp. But if your unemployment benefits have already expired or if the amount is less than you can earn working temporary, you should consider using this tool.

Tool #6: Job Fairs

Pro's: Exposure to multiple companies and/or job vacancies, free or low cost, good networking possibilities

Con's: Can get lost in crowd, some job fairs have poor company representation, visibility may be a problem if currently employed

Job fairs are large scale recruiting events. Their objective is to bring together qualified applicants and company recruiters at one time and in one location, hopefully leading to job offers. These gatherings often attract hundreds, even thousands, of job seekers and may have fifty or more companies represented.

For companies, this method could be cheaper than advertising expenses or personnel agency fees, and more time-efficient as well, since they can screen many applicants in a short period. For you, the job seeker, it offers the advantage of gaining exposure to a number of companies at one time, also saving time and money. In addition, you may encounter companies of which you were not aware or with whom you were unable to make contact.

In the past few years, I have noticed an increase in the number of job fairs offered. Since most of these are free or low cost, you should plan to attend some. Usually these fairs will be advertised in the Sunday help-wanted section of local newspapers or in the weekly events section in the Monday business pages. You also can learn of them through the job networking groups or other job assistance organizations.

Sponsors for these events may be non-profit or for-profit. Typical non-profit sponsors include professional associations, churches, college alumni groups, professional service organizations, industry associations, and local media. Companies that have a large number of positions to fill often will conduct their own "open house" or job fair. In addition to these groups, there are many for-profit firms that conduct job fairs, often for specific target groups (*e.g.*, sales, engineering, ex-military, or computer backgrounds).

Preparation

Much of your preparation will be like preparing for an interview, which of course, is exactly what you are doing. Refer to "Chapter V: Interviewing Techniques" for a full discussion. As with interviewing, your success at the job fair will be largely determined by your planning and preparation. Take time to develop a game plan and start your planning early.

If possible, determine in advance which companies will be present, select the ones with whom you want to interview, and conduct some research into those companies. Rank them in order of importance to you and plan to visit them approximately in that order. The names of the companies planning to attend is usually listed in the display ads in newspapers or other advance notice, but if not, call the sponsor and request the information.

Check ahead for registration requirements or qualifications screening. You may be asked to send in your resume beforehand so that companies can peruse it prior to the event.

Have available many copies of your resume, at least 25. This is one occasion where you will be expected to distribute your resume freely. Of course, be certain it conforms with the principles we discussed earlier in "Chapter III: Preparing Your Resumes."

Carry an attaché case, which will keep your resume neat and clean, as well as have room to store the company literature you will receive. Include a notebook to record your activities or carry a small note pad in your coat pocket.

At the Fair

When you arrive at the fair, you will be given a program of participating companies. In addition to the ones you planned to contact, you may wish to seek out others as well.

Use your time wisely. You may have all day or just a few hours, but either way, you will be at your peak performance for only a few hours at best. Allow time for a short break and to recompose.

Many job fairs also offer seminars on job search techniques, but most of these classes are offered by other groups at other times. (See "Tool

#9: Job Networking Groups.") Your focus should be to make company contacts and to network with other job seekers, and thus I suggest you attend the seminars only after you have completed your mission or as a rest break between interviews.

Make notes regarding each company and their representative with whom you spoke personally, so that you will remember them later. You need not take complete notes, just enough to jog your memory later. You can use this note-taking time as a rest break or when you are waiting in line.

After the Job Fair

Send a thank-you note to the companies with whom you spoke and include some bit of information that will help them remember who you are. They will have spoken with many, many applicants and thus you will need to refresh their memory. In this note, you will indicate that you plan to recontact them in a few days.

In speaking with some company recruiters who have worked at these fairs, a common comment is that applicants must take the initiative in recontacting companies with whom they left their resume or interviewed. If you have mailed a thank-you note, you will have said that you will recontact them; definitely do so.

Evaluate your results from the fair. What did you gain from the experience? What could you have done differently that might have produced better payoff?

Review your notes. What companies should you be recontacting? What actions should you take as a consequence of the fair? What follow-up needs tending? Do you have new leads to check?

Networking at Job Fairs

Job fairs offer an excellent opportunity to job network with other job seekers. For example, while standing in line, you can compare job search techniques and information with the people around you. Anyone you happen to meet is a potential source for leads. Use your "30-second resume" whenever you have the chance.

Save your resumes for the companies, but hand out your business cards freely and solicit others as well; you may wish to contact later

JOB FAIR CHECK LIST

Before the fair
√ Check registration requirements.
√ Determine location.
√ Research companies represented.
√ Prioritize companies to interview.
√ Pack and organize supplies:
    √ Resume in attaché case
    √ Business cards
    √ Small note pad
    √ Breath mints
√ Plan attire.

At the fair
√ Visit most important companies first.
√ Take short breaks and refresh appearance.
√ Network at every opportunity.
√ Exchange business cards.
√ Use breath mints.

After the fair
√ Sort business cards.
√ Review and expand notes.
√ Send thank-you notes
√ Recontact company representatives.
√ Plan follow-up.
√ Evaluate your performance and success

some people that you meet. Don't just mill around waiting for an interview; use all of your time constructively.

Standing Out

As I stated earlier, there may be hundreds or thousands of job seekers at a job fair. How can you stand out from the crowd?

• Develop a game plan for what you plan to do at the fair, using the check list illustrated here, and proceed accordingly. Not only will you accomplish more, but you also will feel less stressed and more relaxed with this preparation. Not surprisingly, you also will reflect that feeling and attitude.

• Be appropriately attired, with a professional, business image. Since you may be there several hours, plan to "freshen up" while there. For example, men should carry an electric shaver in their attaché case and women who wear make-up should also check their appearance often. Carry and use breath mints.

• Be organized. Don't fumble for papers or a resume, but have your materials readily accessible. Keep your business cards in a pocket easy to reach.

• Be prepared. If you know which companies you will be seeing, compile and learn information about them and be certain to relate it during your interview. Prepare for the interview, following all of the suggestions I have outlined in the next chapter on interviewing techniques.

• Take an occasional rest break, so that you will not seem tired.

Conclusion

Why attend job fairs? Depending on the size of the fair, several hundred participants may receive offers then or later from the companies they met or interviewed. Since these events are inexpensive and closeby, you have every reason to attend! This tool is still one more of the many you have learned about through the **CAREER SEARCH SYSTEM**.

Tool #6: Government

Pro's: Generally stable and secure. Local and many state jobs are generally permanent locations. Many openings for recent grads.

Con's: Can be very long and complex procedures. Not good source if you need a job quickly, although efforts are underway to streamline federal hiring.

There are more than 163,000 government employees in the Triangle and Triad areas combined The approximate numbers are these:

	Triangle	Triad
Federal -	8,800	5,600
State -	60,400	12,300
Local -	37,000	39,200

If at all possible, I suggest you go to the local office of your state's employment services agency, which in North and South Carolina is called the Employment Security Commission (ESC). You will find not only local and other North Carolina openings, but federal and local job lists as well.

There is one ESC office in each county throughout North Carolina. The Triangle-Triad locations are as follows; call for directions:

- Raleigh: 700 Wade Avenue, (919) 733-3941
- Durham: 1105 Briggs Avenue, (919) 560-6880
- Greensboro: 2005 S. Elm-Eugene St., (910) 334-5777
- Winston-Salem: 630 W. 6th Street, (910) 761-1700

You will need to carry identification, either your social security card or driver's license. You will be asked if you are an American citizen, and if you are not, then you must provide valid work permit papers.
If you are not able to go to a local branch of the North Carolina Employment Security Commission, then

(1) go to your local state employment services office (or a US Office of Personnel Management, if your city has one) and request the Federal Job Opportunities List. In other states, ask for the North Carolina list and peruse for positions in the Triangle and Triad cities);

(2) while at the employment services office, ask for the North Carolina Employment Security Commission list of current openings and peruse for local openings;

(3) contact the local government offices listed at the end of this section.

U. S. (Federal) Government

The process for obtaining a federal job is somewhat complex, and that is why I urge you to go to your local employment services office. They should be able to explain the procedures involved and help you with the applications. If you still have questions, call the Federal Information Center.

For recorded information convenient by phone, call the Career America Connection at (912) 757-3000. By calling this number, you can obtain current employment and career information, job availability in a specific state and by category, application forms, and materials relating to all government employment. You must call from a "touch-tone" phone, and have pen and paper ready to record information..

If your city has a US Office of Personnel Management (OPM), you can go there and request the Federal Job Opportunities List, which includes all federal job vacancies, broken down by locality. Each OPM has a self-service Federal Job Information Center, open Monday through Friday, from 9 - 4. There is generally an OPM in every state, although the OPM office in Raleigh covers both Carolinas; for other OPM offices, call the Federal Information Center and press "5" with a touch-tone phone. If you do not have an OPM convenient, the same information can be obtained through the state employment assistance offices.

Most federal government agencies hire through the Office of Personnel Management (OPM), formerly known as the civil service commission, and a competitive exam is required. This exam may be all written, all experience-oriented, or a combination of both. You can obtain information on application procedures, application forms, and the Federal Job Opportunities List at many locations, including the employment services offices in all states (there are 150± throughout the Carolinas), college placement departments, and the offices of all members of Congress. These sources will be the fastest methods of obtaining the information, but if none of these sources is available to you, you can write the OPM Raleigh Area Office and request application information and the Federal Job Opportunities List to be mailed to you. I am told this office is extremely busy, and thus use the other sources when possible. Their address is

U S Office of Personnel Management
Raleigh Area Office
P O Box 25069
Raleigh, NC 27611.

Do *not* call. All requests for information must be in writing.

US Postal Service: Certain federal organizations fill their job vacancies through their own hiring systems, and have no contact with OPM. One of the largest of these is the US Postal Service (USPS). For specific employment information, call the District Human Resources office at (910) 668-1252. For recorded information on job vacancies, examination dates, and the procedure to follow, call the job information lines listed here:
> Triangle (919) 831-3653
> Triad (910) 271-5573

Interestingly, nearly all USPS employees start as clerks or carriers, and only the highest levels and technical positions (attorneys, engineers, etc.) are hired from outside the system. Thus, one would start entry-level, and then bid for higher-level positions after one year of employment. All entry-level candidates must take the postal examination, and numerous college grads are hired each year into this program.

Administrative Careers with America: In addition to the above organizations and procedures, the Federal Government's new program Administrative Careers With America (ACWA) is an alternative and usually faster method for obtaining entry-level federal employment, GS 5 - 7 levels. About 100 different types of occupations are filled through this program, and you may apply for these jobs when you are within nine months of graduation, or upon completion of the qualifying academic courses or three years' work experience.

There are two options for applying:

- You may take a written examination. Based on your exam rating, your name will be placed on a list of eligible applicants and referred to Federal agencies with vacancies.

- You may apply based on your college grade-point average (GPA) or scholastic record, without having to take a written exam. To do this, you must be a college graduate and have a GPA of 3.5 (4.0 scale) or higher, for all completed undergraduate course work; or have graduated in the upper ten percent of your class.

Outstanding Scholar Authority: Federal agencies with vacancies can hire recent graduates with a GPA of 3.5+ (on a 4.0 scale) or who have graduated in the top 10% of their class, directly from the outside, bypassing OPM. This can happen when a government recruiter interviews you on campus or you can apply directly to federal agencies for employment consideration. The OPM is establishing an Applicant Referral List, which will contain the names of candidates who meet the GPA/scholastic requirements, but usage of the Referral List by individual agencies is strictly optional. Thus, your best bet is to contact each agency directly, a sizable task. Again, your state employment assistance office can help with addresses of the largest agencies in your area.

For more information regarding ACWA, as well as other government employment, call the Career America Connection (912-757-3000), which I described earlier in this section.

My contact at OPM also suggests that you first write OPM, indicating your objectives and qualifications, and they will send you information regarding the agencies that may have openings for you.

Incidentally, the federal government offers its employees alternative work schedules, one of which allows an employee to work nine-hour days, Monday - Thursday, and then have Friday afternoon free. It's still a 40-hour week, but the half-day can make a nice, long weekend! This schedule is also finding favor within the private sector.

State of North Carolina

There is no central personnel office hiring for all state agencies. Rather, each agency conducts its own personnel recruiting, and you will need to apply to each one in which you have an interest. However, the North Carolina Employment Security Commission will have information on all agencies' current openings and how to apply for them. In addition, they recently have installed a "user-friendly" computer system that will access all the current job openings they have listed, private sector as well as federal, state, and local government agencies.

You cannot obtain a list of NC government openings by mail. Rather, you must go to your local employment services office anywhere in the US (*e.g.*, an Employment Security Commission office in North Carolina) and tell them you are interested in finding employment in a specific locale. They should have all the lists there and can help you apply. However, not all North Carolina vacancies are sent to out-of-state employment service offices, and thus you should go to the one in state if at all possible.

Local Government

Information regarding employment and hiring procedures for the cities and counties in the Triangle and Triad is found in Appendix F, along with federal and state of North Carolina agencies.

A final reminder regarding all government jobs, in North Carolina or anywhere else. The simplest way to learn about and apply for any government job is to visit your local state employment services office and seek their help. They should have the information you need, or they can obtain it easier than you can.

PART 2:

JOB NETWORKING

Tool #8: Developing a Job Network

Tool #9: Job Network Groups

Tool #10: Professional and Trade Associations

Tool #11: The Information Interview

Tool #8: Developing a Job Network

Pro's: Most effective source overall. Works well for all experience levels, especially middle level. Best source for individuals changing fields, re-entering work force, or other difficult-to-place situations.

Con's: Slow, time-consuming, labor intensive, lots of "dead-end" leads.

I am often asked what is the most important part of a job search. The answer is easy: Job Networking!

Looking at all the "con's" to job networking might make you want to skip it, in favor of the easier and simpler methods. Before you do, consider this: More people find their jobs through networking than through any other source, at least 70%, and I have heard estimates of up to 85%! Perhaps this is a good example of the old adage, "You get what you pay for," because even though it is the most difficult, it is the most fruitful.

In addition, twice as many new jobs are generated by smaller businesses than by the large, major companies. In fact, the "Fortune 500" are projected to decrease employment during the current decade, and a recent report by Dun & Bradstreet Corp. indicates that companies with fewer than 100 employees will account for almost 80% of the new jobs. Further, firms with fewer than 20 employees are expected to add 57% of the new positions. As I stated earlier in this chapter, simply mailing your resume to the biggest companies will not find enough openings. Networking, however, will help you locate these smaller firms.

There are several approaches to job networking, all of which can generate many leads and interviews. This and the following three sections detail the most successful methods that you can incorporate in your job search.

Before starting to network, you already must have developed your "30-Second Resume," described in Part 2 of Chapter III. If for some reason, you skipped that discussion, refer back to it now. I stated that you will be using this oral resume often, and now is still another of those times. The "30-second resume" is just as important as your written one, so spend enough time to make it the best possible.

Developing A Job Network

Since job networking can be so productive, you should spend at least half of your time developing this source. I know what you are thinking: that it's too difficult or that you lack the skills or contacts from which to establish your base. Not true – once you get started, you will be surprised how well it goes. As with so much of your job search, it simply requires planning and organization. Even if you are new to the area, you can cultivate a network system; the procedure is the same.

First, let me emphasize what job networking is <u>not</u>. It is not an excuse to abuse your friends and relatives by bombarding them with constant calls for contacts or by pressuring them to use their influence when you sense their reluctance. Certainly you will want to include them in your job networking, but there are so many potential networking sources at your disposal that you should not test the patience of any person. If you find yourself calling the same people, then you are not conducting a correct job search.

Start developing your job network by compiling a list of individuals you want to contact. Begin with friends and relatives, who should be the most sympathetic and supportive, and this will get you off to a good start. Expand this list to include business associates, then social, professional, civic, and church contacts, and anyone else you think could help. However, if you are currently employed and discretion is utmost, you may wish to contact only close, trusted associates.

In compiling this list you also should predetermine why you are including each person. How can they help you? What information do you think they may be able to share with you?

Now phone each one and let them know that you are actively seeking new employment. Conduct your calls seated at the desk of the new "job search area" you have set up, so you can record all of the information you are given and keep it organized. Here are some questions to ask:

- "Do you have any job search suggestions?" They may have just completed a job search themselves and will have some good advice.

Or they may know of someone else who has, and you can contact that person to ask what he/she learned during the job search.

• "Do you have any contacts that could be of assistance?" Perhaps your contact may be friends with a Director of Human Resources that could be a good lead, or a department manager in the field you are seeking, or some other person who might be helpful.

• "Is there a career consultant, personnel agent, or advisor you know and would recommend?"

• "Are you aware of any organized professional associations or job networking groups that I should contact?" (Networking groups, professional associations, and privately funded job-search organizations are all discussed later in this chapter.)

In addition to your initial list, there are many other networking sources. When at social gatherings, listen out for people who might be able to lead you to a source. Call the appropriate academic department head at a local college and ask for suggestions. If possible, discuss your situation with current or former clients.

When you prepared your written resume, you secured at least three persons who agreed to be your references. Definitely include them in your network list, and since they are familiar with the quality of your work, they likely will be able to suggest other persons to contact.

College alumni groups are an outstanding source, and you should locate the local chapter president of your alumni association and attend the meetings, planning to job network there. If you don't know who the local officers are, call the alumni office or the president's office at your alma mater and ask for the local contact.

Many college alumni associations sponsor career seminars and job fairs, and they often have "young alumni" sub-groups. Try to locate alumni with backgrounds similar to yours and ask for career and job search advice. You also should discuss your job search with the chapter president and perhaps arrange an "information interview."[1] In fact, I just spoke with an applicant who expects a job offer from Coca-Cola and whose interview was arranged through the president of his alumni association.

---

[1] The "information interview" is discussed later in this chapter as Tool #9.

Still another valuable source of leads and contacts can be found through professional and trade associations. If you are already a member of a society that covers your field, you should contact the president or job coordinator. In researching this subject, I encountered many persons who obtained their jobs by networking at these monthly meetings, and thus I strongly urge you to try it also. This source is discussed in more detail in the next section, "Tool #10: Professional and Trade Associations," and Appendix E includes information on many of the most active of these groups locally.

If you are contemplating a career change, these professional groups can be a tremendous help. Search out the one(s) that pertain to your newly chosen field, contact them and attend their meetings.

Volunteer your time with a professional association, church, civic group, favorite charity, or any other organization where you will meet people. As you get to know these new friends, they may have suggestions or contacts, and you likely will find persons who recently conducted their own job search. This is especially helpful if you are unemployed, since it keeps you active and involved, as well as adding to your emotional support systems and avoiding depression.

As you see, networking has infinite possibilities. Think about it, and you surely will come up with many more potential sources for contacts.

Conclusion

Don't expect instant results or that all of your efforts will be productive. Accept the fact that although most of your leads will not be useful, you must follow through on all of them anyway. That is the slow, time-consuming part of job networking.

But since networking is the most effective source overall, you should plan to spend much of your time cultivating leads and contacts, and then following through on them. Don't let all the dead ends depress you; sooner or later, one or more of your leads will bear fruit. It only takes the one "right" lead to land you your new job!

Thus, approach each network contact as though an opening were available for you. You never know when there really might be.

CASE EXAMPLE

I recently received a phone call from an accountant who had just located a new job, and since it is a great example of job networking, I want to share it with you.

John had joined the volunteer auxiliary of a well-know charity and then volunteered to assist the group's treasurer during their annual fundraiser. In real life, the treasurer was the Controller with a large corporation, and he was so impressed with John's enthusiasm and abilities, he arranged an interview with his firm for a position in his department. With this recommendation, John was offered a job there!

All non-profit organizations need volunteers. Choose one that you enjoy and then actively participate, especially in a function that will allow you to demonstrate your skills and abilities. It will keep you current in your field, and you will make many new friends and contacts – one of whom may be the source of your next job!

Tool #8: Job Networking Groups

Pro's: Most are free or little expense; offer emotional support, job search seminars, and sometimes job openings; excellent networking opportunity; good source for recent grads through middle-management.

Con's: Some volunteer instructors are not well-qualified; not best source for senior executives; very open and thus may not be good if you are currently employed.

The Triangle and Triad area is fortunate to have several networking groups specifically aimed for job searchers. At any given weekly meeting, you may be introduced to top executives, blue-collar workers, recent college graduates, and everything in between. All are free or very low cost, and no reservations are needed.

While their primary purpose is to help job seekers through job networking, they also offer seminars on the practical aspects of getting a job (*e.g.*, interviewing, resume preparation, focusing your job objective, planning a job search, job networking, etc.). In addition, they maintain files of job openings sent to them by many metro employers, and these files can be perused at the weekly meetings.

In the past few years, I have spoken with many job-seekers who were very pleased with the assistance they received from these organizations, and so I urge you to attend the meetings. Telephone ahead for directions and to confirm times. You may also wish to inquire what topics are being discussed, and plan to attend the one(s) that would be most helpful to you. Although some meet in local churches, they are non-sectarian and all are welcome.

Triangle Area Groups

- *Carolina Job Network:* Sulf-supported job networking group for professionals in transitin. Meets noon every Monday at Raphael Hall (5801 Falls of Neuse Road, Raleigh). A $2 donation is expercted at each meeting. For information, all (919) 990-2468

- *Triangle Job Network:* General job networking groups, meets every Monday from 5:30 - 7:30 pm at the Durham Employment Security Commission)1105 Briggs Avenue, Durham). For more information, contact Linda Vanaman at (919) 489-7664.

- *Triangle Network Group:* Self-supported network group for the Triangle. Meets 8:30 a.m. on second and fourth Wednesday of each month at Brig's Restaurant (Hwy 55, Research Triangle Park). For more information, call Lem Kornegay at (919) 564-0400 x157.

Triad Area Groups

- *Triad Job Search Network:* Member-led networking and support group for the unemployed and underemployed. Meets noon every Tuesday at the Covenant Methodist Church (1526 Skeeet Club Rd, High Point). Cost $2 per meeting to attend. For more information, call (910) 333-1677.

- *Triad Networks Group:* Progressive job networking group. Meets 7:15 am every Wednesday at the J&S Cafeteria (601 Milner Drive, Greensboro). Call (910) 854-1694 for information.

- *Truax Consulting Group:* Private networking group providing networking opportunities, spouse relocation assistance, resume reviews, and other services. Meets at 5:45 pm first and third Wednesday monthly at 2102 N. Elm St., Suite K1 in Greensboro. For more information, contact Bonnie Truax at (910) 271-2050.

- *Professionals in Transition:* A non-profit job hunting support group offering networking opportunities and job hunting tips. Meets 7:00 pm every Thursday at the American Red Cross Building at 690 Coliseum Drive in Winston-Salem. For more information, Contact Damian Birkel at (910) 924-0818.

- *Greensboro Area Incentives Group (GAIN):* Women'o networking and support group comprised of female executies and business owners. Offers informal job assistance. Meets the last Wednesday of each month for dinner, usually at the Painted Plate (Forum IV, 5th floor, Greensboro). For more information, contact Judith Abraham at (910) 294-1968.

Procedure for attending networking meetings

A little preparation before the meetings and some understanding of the networking opportunities they offer will help you derive the most from these groups.

Plan ahead. Carry a few copies of your resume, but you should give one only to persons who request it. Far better is to pass out your business card, which will show your job objective or expertise and your contact data. This small card is easier to keep and less likely to be tossed in the trash.

Since you may receive more and better information if you project a professional image, I suggest you dress well, although not necessarily in complete business attire. Pay attention to your personnel hygiene and carry breath mints. Needless to say, be certain you know the time, date, and location.

Arrive early. Remember that the primary focus of these groups is to encourage job networking. Arriving 20 minutes early will allow more time to meet other job seekers and exchange information.

Set goals. A easy goal is to meet at least ten attendees and exchange business cards. Discuss what you have learned and ask for suggestions from them. An even better plan is to locate at least two attendees with backgrounds or objectives similar to your own. Trading job hunting tips with them will be especially helpful to your own search, as well as to theirs. Ask for suggestions in selecting personnel agencies.

Don't waste time. Don't spend too much time with one person. Keep moving and try to locate other participants who can address your needs. However, you should always exchange business cards and perhaps phone those persons later. Should you locate someone with very good information relative to your job search, get their name and contact data (a business card, for example) and ask if you can call or meet with them later, when there are fewer distractions and you can continue your dialogue.

Actively participate. Converse with as many people as you have time. If you are researching a specific company and seeking information or a contact there, mention it often. You likely will encounter someone who can help. Many of the classes allot time for this exchange of information and you should mention it then also. If you have questions or comments during the classes, speak up. The facilitators are glad to hear from you, if you don't monopolize their time.

Identify yourself. Each group has a sign-in table and you are given a name tag on which to write your name. Under your name and in only a few words, include your job objective or expertise in letters large enough for other attendees to read. If someone with a background or objective similar to yours sees this tag, you likely will have identified a useful source. For variety, you occasionally might write in your alma mater, home state, former employer, etc.

Take notes. The classes are generally informative, and you should take notes. You also will want to record details about some of the participants you meet and the information you obtain from them.

Exchange information. If everyone at these meetings only selfishly soaked up information from other attendees, there would be no purpose in participating. Offer your own ideas and experiences, and any other information helpful to others. Some weeks you may feel that you have given more than you have received, but it will all balance out later. However, don't allow yourself to be trapped by someone seeking too much information for the short period you have at the meeting. Should this be developing, ask if you can call them later when you both have more time for discussion.

JOB NETWORKING MEETINGS
Check List

Before the meeting
√ Decide attire
√ Plan what to carry and how:
   √ Resumes in folder or attaché
   √ Business cards in pocket
   √ Note pad convenient
√ Rehearse "30-second resume"
√ Confirm time and location
√ Set objectives

At the meeting
√ Arrive early
√ Identify self and job objective
√ Actively participate
√ Achieve goals
√ Don't waste time
√ Take notes
√ Exchange business cards

After the meeting
√ Renew contacts
√ Analyze results
√ Determine follow-up
√ Review notes

Follow-up. All of the knowledge you obtained at the meeting will be useless, unless you incorporate it into your search. In addition, keep in contact with some of the participants you meet, especially those with backgrounds or objectives similar to your own. If someone provided you with information that resulted in some positive step in your search, send them a thank you note.

Conclusion

Although your results will vary from week to week, you will always come away with a boost in morale from commiserating with other job seekers like yourself. I also suggest you occasionally take your spouse or best friend with you, so that they will better understand what you are doing and feel more personally involved.

These groups perform an outstanding service to the local areas and their sponsors are much to be commended. Since they offer so much and are also free, you should include them in your job search.

A word of caution: I have observed that many attendees seem to be hooked on the seminars offered and ignore the opportunity for networking. Although the seminars offered are very helpful indeed, that is only part of your reason for being there. If you only attend the seminars or only speak with your friends there, you will not be profiting from all you should.

Tool #10: Trade and Professional Associations

Pro's: Works well for middle- and upper-level executives, and somewhat for entry-level. Good source for changing careers.

Con's: May be costly if you must join first or pay to attend meetings. Can be slow and time-consuming getting to the source.

Too few job seekers are aware of the excellent job search potential found in their professional associations. Not only do these groups offer excellent opportunities for networking, but also they frequently have well-developed career placement and career enhancement programs, and some even sponsor job fairs. Although not all associations offer these services, those that do can provide a significant boost to your career search.

Association help comes in many ways, including monthly newsletters listing both job seekers and job openings, a resume bank retained for companies to peruse, a job information "hot line," annual job fairs, and direct matching of jobs and applicants. Smaller organizations may have a less formal, yet very effective networking system. In addition, many associations sponsor career development seminars, covering such topics as job search within their industry, career planning, industry innovations, etc.

There is an organization covering virtually every conceivable job description, industry or academic discipline. Although you already may be a member of one or more of these associations, there likely are other associations of which you may not be aware, but from which you could benefit. *National Trade and Professional Associations of the United States* (published by Columbia Books, Inc., Washington, DC) is a catalogue that lists thousands of trade and professional associations and labor unions with national memberships. Even more complete is the *Encyclopedia of Associations*, a multi-volume work that includes detailed information.

Available at most public libraries, these books include not only addresses and descriptions of each organization, but also a cross reference section to access associations by subject. You likely will be surprised to learn that many disciplines are represented by numerous associations, some of which specialize in specific industries. For example, under the Subject Index heading "Marketing," there are 75+ specialty associations, in addition to the 52,000-member American Marketing Association. In the same section, there are many organizations listed for specific ethic or minority groups, such as "black," "women," "handicapped," etc. Thus, I urge you to incorporate these publications in your job search. (If you are not able to obtain these through a local public library, mail order information is included in "Tool #14: Publications.")

Nearly all of the largest associations offer job assistance on the national level. Moreover, I have researched a large number of these groups that offer some sort of job assistance locally, either formal or informal, and included them in Appendix E. If your association is not listed, I suggest that you contact the national headquarters of your association and ask for the local chapter president, and then inquire about their direct career assistance, if any. In future editions, I hope to add still more associations, and I would appreciate hearing from you if you have information on others that are not included in my current list.

In some cases, you must be a member of the association offering employment assistance before they will help you. However, I was pleased to find that many organizations are interested in helping an applicant secure employment now, assuming he/she will join the association later. Since membership dues can be expensive – prohibitively so if you are unemployed – I suggest you call the association contact I have listed to inquire if membership is a prerequisite.

Some associations require a small fee to cover costs, especially if their services are extensive or staffed by volunteers. In some cases, the fee is waived for members. I have noted these charges and other requirements when applicable.
If your association does not offer any formal job assistance, remember that you can attend their meetings and network there; in fact, I have recently spoken with several persons who obtained their current jobs that way. And if the associations do offer job search assistance that you plan to use, you have even more reason for attending their meetings.

Most associations meet monthly and welcome visitors and potential members, in addition to their current members. Since there may be a fee involved or reservations required, you should check ahead. Appendix E also includes information on monthly meeting dates. If you are strapped for cash and don't want to stay for the meal, you can leave after the social hour or the business meeting.

Networking at Association Meetings

A close friend of mine recently moved here in search of an audit/accounting position. I suggested that he attend a meeting of the Institute of Internal Auditors, which he did, and he even sat beside a woman who had just found her job the previous month by networking at the I. I. A. meetings. Unfortunately, however, Ray is somewhat shy and felt uncomfortable in an unfamiliar setting where he knew no one. He spent the entire evening alone and gained nothing from the experience, except a fear of ever returning!

Many job seekers are like Ray, and you may be one of them. With a little preparation beforehand, however, you can overcome your reticence and successfully job network at any meeting – professional association, alumni group, business meeting, or whatever. The key word here is "preparation."

I included the name and phone number of at least two members (the president, job coordinator, and/or membership chairman) of every association listed in Appendix E. You should call one of those officers to confirm the meeting date, place, fee, and program of the next meeting, and then indicate that you would like to attend. Ask if you can meet this officer and/or some other officers at the meeting and if they will introduce you to a few members. If you are unable to stay for the meal, tell your new contact so that the association is not charged for it.

Now set your objectives for the meeting. What do you hope to accomplish? You will want to meet some officers, certainly the president and/or the job coordinator. Ask if there are members who recently completed a job search, and then try to locate them to discuss your current search and to ask for suggestions. Are there other specific members you want to meet, department managers with certain companies, etc.?

Plan what you will wear – business attire, of course. You should dress as though you were going on an interview, which is exactly what

NETWORKING AT
ASSOCIATION MEETINGS
Check List

Before the meeting
√ Set objectives
√ Establish contact(s)
√ Determine time, location, and fees
√ Put business cards and note pad in pocket
  (no folders or attaché cases)
√ Rehearse "30-second resume"
√ Decide attire

At the meeting
√ Meet appropriate officers
√ Achieve objectives
√ Don't spend too much time with one person
√ Volunteer time, if possible
√ Ask open-ended questions and <u>listen</u>
√ Record short notes
√ Exchange business cards rather than pass out
  résumés
√ Keep right hand free for handshakes

After the meeting
√ Expand notes
√ Send thank-you letters
√ Analyze results
√ Determine follow-up
√ What will you do differently at the next
  meeting?

you are doing! Carry enough business cards to hand out, as well as a few resumes to give to key people. Take a small, pocket-size notebook to record quick information. Remember your "30-Second Resume"? You will use it often at the meeting, so rehearse it some more.

At the meeting, remember your objectives. Don't spend too much time with one person, or you may run out of time. Ask open-ended questions, and then listen; people are always more impressed with good listeners than they are with good talkers! Do not pass out too many resumes, three at the most, or you will seem too opportunistic. Record names and information in your notebook, but don't waste time recording too much now; you can do that later.

If you have the inclination and the time available, volunteer to help out on a committee or such. You will make some valuable contacts and begin to feel more comfortable at the meetings.

Immediately after the meeting, record your results. Whom did you meet (name, company, job title, association function, etc.)? What follow-up do you plan? Is there someone you met and with whom you would like to schedule an "information interview"? What would you want to do differently at the next meeting?

You should send a thank-you note to the person who introduced you at the meeting and enclose your business card. Are there others you need to write and/or send a resume?

Planning what you will do at these meetings will make you less nervous and self-conscious, plus you will accomplish more. You can use this procedure to network at other meetings as well (*e.g.*, college alumni groups, social gatherings, etc.) As with so much of your job search, it only takes organization and preparation.

Conclusion

In reviewing "Appendix E: Trade and Professional Associations," you will note that I have included specific names to contact, rather than only titles, as I did in the company list. This is because many organizations are mostly volunteer and not listed in the phone book, and the fastest way to reach them is through a member or officer. However, since these officials are usually elected for one year only, you may be referred to the current slate of officers for help.

I personally know of many people who found their jobs through associations, and so I am positive it works. Definitely plan to incorporate them in your search. In the "Professional Associations" section of your notebook, record the names of the associations you contact, the people with whom you speak, when you attended meetings, and the results. These contacts will be helpful now and later.

After you are employed, I strongly urge you to become active in your association, not only attending the meetings but also volunteering for committees and signing up for professional seminars. The knowledge you will gain from the meetings, programs, and classes will be very helpful in advancing your career, as will the professional contacts you make. Drawing from your own experiences will enable you to be very helpful to other job seekers – and then too, you never know when you might need their services again!

Tool #11: The Information Interview

Pro's: Especially helpful to change careers or re-enter the job market. Good way to re-energize a stale job search campaign. Provides more useful information than can be obtained in informal settings.

Con's: Very time consuming. Can be difficult to find right sources to contact. May not be feasible if you are not in the city where you are attempting to relocate.

The information interview is the current rage among career counselors, and for a good reason: it works!

Essentially, the information interview is contacting successful and knowledgeable business associates or authorities in your field, and arranging a meeting time to discuss your job search face-to-face, rather than over the phone or at some other informal setting. During this interview, you attempt to obtain much of the same information you would have asked on the phone, but now in more depth and with more details.

The primary reason for using this approach is that you are likely to get more and better information in a formal interview setting than you would simply by phone. It is especially helpful if you are contemplating the possibility of changing careers or re-entering the job market, and you want some ideas and information to help you with your decision. It is also useful if you are having a difficult time with your search and need some fresh input and suggestions to get you going again. Even if you don't fit either of those categories, you likely will find this method profitable.

You also can "cold call" a department manager or other executive and request an interview time to discuss your career search. Some managers will be flattered that you consider them an authority and will be glad to talk with you; others, however, may consider it a nuisance.

I even know someone who was able to create his current job with a company that he "cold called" for an information interview! That, however, is the exception and you should not mislead your contact by saying you are seeking help when in fact you want a job interview. Your objective is to gain information – suggestions, names, etc. – and trying to turn your information interview into a job interview will offend your source.

Nevertheless, if you do sense during your discussion that your source is asking questions that suggest you may be considered for a position within the company, be prepared for a full job interview. You should have read "Chapter V: Interviewing Techniques" and thus are ready for this pleasant turn of events!

Although you may think that a luncheon is a good location for an information interview, it really is not. There are too many distractions and the setting is too informal. Try to conduct your interviews in your source's office where you will have his/her undivided attention.

The main disadvantage to the information interview is that it is far more time-consuming than a phone call. If you are currently employed or not living in the same city as your potential sources, you may not be able to utilize this method. In addition, some of your contacts may feel inconvenienced, particularly if they are often called upon for this type of interview. Nevertheless, it is a good networking technique, and I suggest you consider it.

Procedure

To derive the most from this technique, you must – guess what? – organize and prepare. To facilitate this, I have designated six steps to follow.

Step 1: Compile a list. First make a list of persons to contact and why. Or you may need to use the reverse approach, and decide what information you want and then research the name of a specific authority who might have that knowledge.

Since information interviews are time-consuming, you should be selective in planning your list. What possible information can you obtain from each person on your list and how can you use it in your job search? Having answered that, you are ready to call your first authority.

Step 2:   Contact your authorities.   Unless you are contacting a personal friend, you should phone your authorities at their place of employment.   During the conversation, you will state why you are calling (You are seeking information as part of a job search.) and why you are targeting this person (You consider your source to be an expert on some subject related to your job search.).   Immediately state that you are not calling for a job interview, but only for information that will be helpful in your job search.   Then ask for a fifteen minute interview time when it is convenience.

In attempting to reach your sources, you may encounter problems getting through the secretary or receptionist.   Remember that part of these employees' job is to screen unwanted calls for their bosses, so don't be upset if you are quizzed on the purpose of your call.   On the contrary, these assistants can be your ally if approached correctly.

You likely will be asked, "May I say who is calling?" and/or "May I ask to what this is in reference."   Instead of trying all sorts of devious end runs, try to gain support by telling the truth, stressing that you are not seeking a job interview and that you will take up only a minute or two of the boss's time on the phone.   If you have been referred to this authority by someone, say that so-and-so said you should call.   If you are told that your authority is not available now, ask when a convenient time will be to call back.   Be polite, ask the secretary's name, and then thank him/her for the information.   When you do call later, be certain you refer to the secretary by name.

If after several attempts you cannot bypass this roadblock, try calling early in the morning, before normal business hours, or late in the afternoon, after business hours.

Step 3:   Prepare for the interview.   After you have established an interview time, the next step is to plan what you will do in the interview, and understanding your respective roles will help.   Even though you will be seated in the small chair in front of the big desk, nevertheless you are the interviewer now and your victim is the "interviewee."   Thus, you will have prepared just as thoroughly as you would expect from one of your interviewers.

What questions should you ask?   This will depend on why you have arranged the interview and what your objectives are.   Decide what general and specific information you hope to learn, and then develop questions which may lead to that information.

For example, if you are considering a new career, you should ask questions such as these:
- Why did you pursue this career?
- What qualifications did you have for this career?
- What do you like most about your industry? What do you dislike?
- Would you encourage others to pursue this career? Why?
- To what do you attribute your success here? (A nice compliment!)

If you are attempting to further your established career path, these questions could be helpful:
- What do you feel are the future trends in our industry?
- Which companies are experiencing the strongest growth in our field? Who are the "winners" and the "losers"?
- Of which professional associations are you a member? Who are the officers?
- If you were considering a job change, what companies or individuals would you contact?
- Why have you and your company been successful? (Again, a compliment!)

Although you should not carry a notebook and take notes during a job interview, you will do so here, since you are the interviewer. Write your questions in a place that will be easily accessible during the interview (the first page of your notebook, on a separate note card, etc.). During the interview, you also will have spontaneous questions that arise from the conversation.

A day or so before the interview, plan what you will wear – professional attire, of course. Check out the location and be certain you know how to get there. Even still, on the day of the interview, allow extra travel time; there is no excuse for being late.

Step 4: Take charge of the interview. Remember your objective for the interview (to get as much information as possible) and don't waste too much time in incidental conversation. Thank your source for allowing you this time and for sharing this knowledge with you. Then get straight to the point. Your contact will appreciate your time concern and the interview will be off to a good start.

During the interview, don't feel that you must write down every bit of information now. Make the most of this short interview and record just enough information to jog your memory later, realizing your time constraints.

After your allotted time is over, thank your source for the time and information, and then end the interview. Let me repeat this: after your allotted time is over, thank your source and then end the interview. If you overextend and wear out your welcome, your source will be irritated and you will lose any empathy and support you may have developed. However, if you are offered more time, you can accept if you wish.

Step 5: Review the interview. Immediately after the interview is concluded, record the information you did not have time to write during the interview. Then critique your performance. What would you like to have done differently if you had the opportunity? What will you do differently on your next information interview? Did you obtain the information you needed?

Step 6: Plan your follow-up. Now analyze the information you garnered and plan what you will do with it. Do you have new authorities to contact? Did your source mention companies you now wish to call? Are there organizations and/or associations you plan to contact and meetings you plan to attend?

Don't forget to send your source a thank-you note as soon as possible. A hand-written note is fine, if that is more convenient. If you have some item of information that you feel would be of interest, enclose it with your note. Be certain to include your address and phone number or a business card, should he/she recall some information later for you.

You may wish to stay in touch with this specialist periodically. If so, note on your calendar when you should call back, probably in a few weeks. Needless to say, don't become a pest!

Carrying your resume

Should you carry your resume to an information interview? There are two theories on this, and since both have merit, use the approach that suits you.

You may have a copy of your resume, in case your source asks for it, but do not offer it yourself. Remember that you are there to obtain information to use in your job search, and offering your resume will both waste time that you could better use asking questions, as well as possibly offend your source who is expecting an information interview only.

Nevertheless, if during the interview, your source is impressed with your preparation, thoroughness, and/or subject knowledge, you may be considered for possible employment. Having your resume then allows you to seize this opportunity.

The other approach is *not* to carry a resume with you. If asked for it, state that you did not bring one, since you are only conducting an information interview. Then offer to bring one by later. This way, you may be able to have two interviews, one for information and another for possible employment.

Conclusion

How successful this technique works for you will be determined by

> 1) how successful you are in selecting good sources to interview,

> 2) how well you prepare for the interview, and

> 3) how much use you make from the information you are given.

I am often called for an information interview, and I know from these experiences that the information I recall during the session is much better than that I would have given on the phone. People generally like to be helpful (especially when there is no tangible cost involved!), and I think you will be pleasantly surprised with the reception you receive. Even if your source is reluctant to have a personal interview, you will probably be given helpful information on the phone.

INFORMATION INTERVIEW
Check List

Before the interview
√ Determine objectives
√ Plan questions
√ Decide attire
√ Carry resume?
√ Have business cards convenient
√ Carry folder, not attaché case

During the interview
√ Take charge of interview
√ Remember and complete objectives
√ Don't waste time
√ Take short notes
√ End interview on time

After the interview
√ Critique performance
√ Expand notes
√ Send thank-you letter
√ Plan follow-up

PART 3:

OTHER RESOURCES

Tool #12: Public Agencies

Tool #13: Privately Funded Organizations

Tool #14: Useful Publications

Tool #12: Public Agencies

Pro's: Free and easy source. Free testing and counseling available. Listings at all levels of experience. Includes jobs available in the public and private sectors.

Con's: Companies tend to shy away from public agencies, since there is limited applicant screening or matching.

Job Service Centers

The Employment Security Commission of North Carolina operates 80 Job Service Centers throughout the state, and maintains lists of job openings from corporations, state and local governments, and many federal agencies. At your request, a trained counselor will administer and evaluate a battery of aptitude tests (up to 4 1/2 hours long!) and occupational interest tests. In addition, they offer information on the procedure to follow in applying for state and federal government positions.

The Triangle-Triad locations are as follows; call for directions:

- Raleigh: 700 Wade Avenue, (919) 733-3941
- Durham: 1105 Briggs Avenue, (919) 560-6880
- Greensboro: 2005 S. Elm-Eugene St., (910) 334-5777
- Winston-Salem: 630 W. 6th Street, (910) 761-1700

If you are not in the Triangle/Triad area, you can obtain most of the same information by visiting your local employment service center anywhere in the US, and requesting that they obtain the information from the North Carolina Employment Security Commission; most likely, they already will have it.

State-Supported Colleges

University of North Carolina at Chapel Hill (UNC-CH): The placement office of state-supported UNC-CH is primarily focused on helping graduating seniors at the university, and thus offers only limited direct assistance to other job seekers. However, their career information library is open for anyone to do research.

Their address is
UNC-CH Career and Placement Services
211 Hanes Hall, Chapel Hill, NC 27599-5140.
(919) 962-6507

North Carolina State University (NCSU): As with UNC-CH, the NCSU career center primarily helps graduating seniors and alumni. In fact, the staff is so busy helping students and the career library so full, that this probably is not a helpful resource.

Their address is
NCSU Career Center
P O Box 7303, Raleigh, NC 27695.
(919) 515-2011 or 515-2396

Veterans' Placement Unit

Federal law mandates that each state must have a special job assistance program for veterans, and each state employment office will have at least one veteran (often a disabled veteran) on staff responsible for administering this program.

If you are a veteran and wish to participate in this service, you must visit one of the many state employment offices (no appointment necessary) and complete an veteran's application form. Then you will be assigned to a job counselor, who will offer job-search advice, make job development phone calls in your behalf, and attempt to arrange employment interviews.

Tool #13: Privately Funded Organizations[1]

Pro's: Specialized help for specific target groups. Will more closely empathize with your problems. Often acts as non-profit personnel agency, arranging interviews, counseling, etc.

Con's: Often must be "minority" group member. Companies tend to shy away from non-selective referrals.

Winston-Salem Urban League

The Employment Services Division of the Winston-Salem Urban League provides comprehensive counseling and services for persons seeking employment and job skills training opportunities. They also offer job search assistance and placement, and they work with prospective employers in search of personnel. Although the service is open for all, most of their applicants are African-American.

For more information, contact the Urban League at
201 W. 5th Street, Winston-Salem, NC 27101
(910) 725-5614

Triangle J Council of Gevernments – Area Agency on Aging

Funded by the United Way, this organization offers numerous job assistance programs for people over age 55. Besides regular job skills classes, they offer two employment programs. The Senior Community Service for Employment offers entry-level part-time jobs to low income individuals. The Senior Environmental Employment Program offers 25 full-time positions wih the EPA in the Research Triangle, usually for

---

[1] See also "Tool #9: Job Network Groups," discussed earlier in this chapter.

engineer technicians and office support. This agency is also aware of other jobs outside of these two programs.

For more information, contact them at
100 Park Drive, P O Box 12276,
Research Triangle Park, NC 27709
(919) 549-0551

The Women's Center

Also funded by the United Way, this non-profit support group in Raleigh offers a number of services to women including job search assistance. They offer self-help seminars, a resource library, and referrals. For further information, call (919) 829-3711. The address is

128 E. Hargett Street, Raleigh 27601.

Southeast Employment Network

Unlike the other network groups I discussed earlier, this is not an "applicant-oriented" network. Rather, it is a private group of 80± technical recruiters representing mostly high tech companies with facilities throughout the Southeast. They meet monthly to discuss the personnel needs of their individual companies and to share resumes they have received, as well as any other helpful recruiting information. If your background is in MIS, high-tech engineering or telecommunications, or your objective is computer systems-oriented, or you have a non-technical background but have worked in a technical environment (*e.g.*, human resources for a high tech company), you can have your resume circulated to all 80± member companies simply by mailing one copy to

Barry Jones
P O Box 2404, Lilburn, GA 30247
(404) 921-0751

Tool #14: Useful Resources and Publications

Pro's: Sources smaller, specialized companies for specific industry experience, as well as larger corporations and employers. Most helpful for experienced applicants searching for companies in their industry.

Con's: Moderate expense or travel to a public library, some duplication from other sources.

I am including information on reference materials that you may order, although many are available at public libraries, and some comments regarding each.

Chambers of Commerce

Several helpful publications are available from the five Chambers of Commerce covering the Triangle-Triad region.

- Raleigh Chamber of Commerce (919) 644-7000:
    Directory of Major Employers in Wake County ($19.50)
    Order via phone with Visa/MC, or write to
    PO Box 2978, Raleigh NC 27602
    Attn: Information Center.

- Durham Chamber of Commerce (919) 682-2133:
    Directory of Organizations Employing Over 100 ($13)
    Order by phone with Visa/MC, or write to
    P O Box 3892, Durham, NC 27702.

- Greensboro Chamber of Commerce (910) 275-8675:
    Guilford County Major Employers Directory ($11)
    Order by phone with Visa/MC, or write to
    P O Box 3246, Greensboro, NC 27402

- Winston-Salem Chamber of Commerce (910) 725-2361
  Major Employers Directory ($12)
  Send check with additional $3 postage/handling to
  P O Box 1408, Winston-Salem, NC 27102

- Research Triangle Foundation (RTP) (919) 549-8181
  Directory of RTP Owners and Tenants
  Call to receive FREE copy of this useful guide which explains the nature of all RTP companies and usually lists their executives.

Periodicals:

Business North Carolina is a monthly business magazine owned by Raleigh's *The News & Observer*. For subscription information, call (704) 523-9560, or write
  5435 77 Center Drive, Suite 50, Charlotte, NC 28217.

Business Life is a monthly business magazine for the Triad area, and contains a helpful section called "Start-Ups and Expansions" that lists new and growing companies. Call (910) 854-4260, or write
  3409-J West Wendover Avenue, Greensboro, NC 27407.

North Carolina is a monthly business magazine published by the NC Citizens for Business and Industry, and focuses more on industrial firms. Call (919) 828-0758, or write PO Box 2508, Raleigh 27602.

Book of Lists

The *Triangle Business Journal* produces an annual publication called the *Book of Lists*, which includes the 25 or so largest companies in various categories, and information about their sales, number of employees, major clients, etc. It is interesting reading in general, and it could be helpful to you to locate companies within a specific industry or profession. The current edition lists 50+ categories, including a list of the largest RTP companies and the 50 fastest growing Triangle companies.

To order, send $15.00 (or $99 for computer disc) to
  Biz Books, Inc.
  128 S. Tryon Street, Suite 2200, Charlotte, NC 28202
  Order by phone at (704) 371-3289 and charge to Visa, MC, Amex.

The *Triad Business News* publishes a similar directory, although somewhat smaller in scope, for $10. Send check to *Triad Business News* at PO Box 18249, Greensboro, NC 27419, or call (910) 854-3001 to order by phone.

Physicians' Desk Reference (PDR)

The primary focus of this weighty book is to provide doctors with detailed information on all prescription drugs. In addition, it lists drug manufacturers, complete with the addresses and phone numbers of their corporate headquarters and regional offices, and even includes the names and contact data for their sales and operations managers. If you are seeking a job in some medical field, either sales or management, the PDR will supply you with names to contact and information on the products marketed by each company. The PDR is available at most public libraries, or if you have a friend who is a doctor or who works in a medical facility, you probably can borrow one.

National Trade and Professional Associations of the U. S.

I made reference to this catalogue in "Tool #10: Professional and Trade Associations." It is available at most public libraries, but you may order it if you wish. Send $48.00 (postpaid) to
Columbia Books, Inc., Publishers
1350 New York Ave NW, Suite 207
Washington, DC 20005-3286.

State Manufacturers Registers

Lists thousands of manufacturers, with contact data, sales figures, size, primary executives (including personnel, accounting managers, engineering managers, etc.), import status, brand of computer and more. You can order a copy for $100±, but I suggest you reference the free public library instead.
Manufacturers' News, Inc.
1633 Central Street
Evanston, IL 60201-9729
(708) 864-7000 – To order directory on IBM disk

CHAPTER V

STEP FOUR:

INTERVIEWING TECHNIQUES

CHAPTER V

Step Four: Interviewing Techniques

Congratulations!

The fact that you are being given an interview indicates that you obviously have presented yourself well so far and that the interviewer has at least some interest in you to grant you some of his/her time. You have worked hard to get to this point, but don't let up yet.

Preparation

Remember this quotation:

> "The successful job-seeker is the one who is willing to do what the unsuccessful will not: Preparation."

Preparation is important in every part of your job search, and it is absolutely essential to a successful interview. Nervous? That could be because you haven't adequately prepared! Being prepared not only settles the stomach, it impresses the interviewer as well.

Research the company, and when possible, research the job and in-terviewer. Learn as much about the company as timely possible, but don't feel that you must know more than the interviewer. Here is the basic information to digest:

• Most importantly, know the company's products or services. What do they offer, provide, manufacture, or sell?

• What is their annual growth and how profitable are they?

• What can you find out about their industry in general, including competitors?

• What is their ranking within their industry?

• Research the company's history.

• Try to determine their reputation. Are they considered aggressive? What is their personnel turnover rate? How are they regarded by their customers? This information is subjective and may be difficult to obtain, but if you have a reliable source, it is good information to know.

• Every corporation has its individual "culture," a nebulous term to describe a company's philosophy, attitudes, dress codes, and the image it strives to project. Knowing these factors can direct you with your answers and behavior during the interview.

• Find out as much as you can about the interviewer(s), especially background and previous employment, interviewing techniques, hobbies, interests, etc. If your interview was arranged through an intermediary, that person may be able to relay good insight into the whims of the interviewer(s); good personnel agencies always should have this information.

Researching most of the company data is easy, and there are many sources. The simplest method is to call the company and ask for an annual report, information brochure, or recruiting information to be mailed to you. If the company declines, as many privately-held companies will, or if you are short on time, go to your college placement center or the public library. Some good reference books include *Standard and Poor's, Moody's, Million Dollar Directory, American Corporate Families* and *Thomas Register of American Manufacturers.* All of these publications are readily available in the business reference section in the larger branches of public libraries.

Networking is also a good source. Ask friends or business contacts if they are familiar with the company; however, keep in mind you may be hearing biased information or rumor, and treat this information accordingly. If you know some of the company's clients, you can carefully and discreetly call them for information.

Anticipate certain questions and be ready with your answers. I recently spoke with a Vice President of Human Resources who told me that for his last job search, he wrote down fifty questions an interviewer might ask. Then he wrote down his answers, and put it aside for a few days. Reading them later, he realized how bad some of his answers really were, and he thought them through again. That took a lot of time – but then too, his thoroughness paid off in a big way!

It is impossible to anticipate every question you might be asked, but knowing what your interviewers are seeking with their questions will help you plan your responses. Of course, you must have the technical expertise required for the position. Excluding that, interviewers look for three primary factors:

1) Clear and certain job focus. You know what job you are currently seeking and how it fits into your career plans.

2) Your life patterns – that is, demonstrated patterns of success, accomplishment, over-achievement, etc., and the opposites.

3) Your ability to "sell yourself" – that is, convincing the interviewer you are the one to hire! In my experiences, more applicants are rejected for failing this, than for any other reason.

The following characteristics are ones most often rated by an interviewer. Read these through several times, and think how they may be asked to you and how you will respond to best "sell yourself."

Intelligence: Conceptual ability, breadth of knowledge, verbal expression, organized thoughts, analytical thought process, logical decision-making.

Decisiveness: Non-ambivalence, willingness to commit self when asked, makes definite choices, lets you know where he/she stands on issues, not tentative.

Energy and Enthusiasm: Animated, spontaneous, fast-paced throughout, positive attitude, optimistic outlook.

Results-orientation: Responses revolve around task accomplishment, gets to the point, emphasizes achievements, provides information relevant to interview objectives, able to give specific instances and examples.

Maturity: Acceptance of responsibility for one's actions, poised, self-confident, appropriately dressed, relaxed, ability to reflect on experiences, understands strengths and weaknesses, clear career goals.

Assertiveness: Responds in a forceful manner, does not ramble, speaks in a convincing tone, persuasive, good at selling self and ideas, good communicator.

Sensitivity: Sincere, friendly, tactful, responsive, not aloof, listens as well as speaks, asks relevant questions.

Openness: Discusses short-comings as well as strengths, is not pre-occupied with saying the right thing, consistent responsiveness regardless of content.

Tough-mindedness: Stands up to interviewer when there is disagreement, discusses persons and events critically, does not allow emotions to cloud perceptions.

The "Stress Interview"

I recently read an article stating that the so-called "stress interview" is becoming popular again. It has been around for as many years as I have been in personnel, but had fallen into disfavor because of its basically negative approach. According to the article, however, in today's stressful business environment, companies would like to put you in a stress situation and then judge how well you can perform. Although I doubt you will encounter this style of interviewing often, you should be prepared in the event you do.

In a stress interview, the interviewer will appear to disagree with nearly everything you say, in order to see how you react. His/her comments, questions, and general body language are geared to lead you astray, to offer you opportunities to make mistakes, and to generally make you uncomfortable. Oftentimes, the interviewer will ask a question, and then after you have given your answer, will sit quietly as though expecting you to continue.

If you sense you are in this type of interview, stick to your guns, and above all, do not begin to contradict yourself or start to ramble in a vain attempt to please the interviewer. In particular, once you have answered a question to your own satisfaction, stop and wait for the interviewer to continue; in my practice, I have had many applicants rejected because they didn't know when to stop talking.

Interviewing Tips

Over the years, interview styles and questions have changed. Many years ago, the vogue questions were "What are your strengths?" and conversely, "What are your weaknesses?" Until recently, "Tell me about yourself" was the technique of choice, and it continues to be very popular with many interviewers. Although you will still encounter those questions, the current fad in interviewing now revolves around open-ended questions asking for specific examples or instances: "Give me an example of how you . . . ."

The following are frequently asked questions that you should anticipate and for which you should have planned an answer:

1) How did you choose your college? Why did you choose your major? What did you intend to do with that degree?

2) Why did you leave your past employers?

3) Pick three adjectives to describe yourself.

4) Give me a specific example of a problem you overcame in your job.

5) What are the qualities of a good manager [salesperson, accountant, engineer, etc.]?

6) How would you rate your success with your job? Why were you successful?

7) What did you like [or dislike] most about your last job? If you could change anything about your last job, what would it be?

147

8) Rank these in order of preference: salary, location, nature of the job.

9) Where do you expect to be in your career in five years?

10) Tell me about yourself.

11) What do you consider the major accomplishment(s) or achievements(s) in your life and/or career?

12) Give me an example of an unpopular policy you had to implement and how you did it.

13) Why are you considering a job change?

14) Evaluate your present and past supervisors. (Recent grads may be asked to evaluate their instructors.)

15) Why haven't you found a job after so many months?

16) What interests you about this job?

17) What can you contribute to our organization?

18) How well do you communicate with others? Give me an example of a communications problem you encountered and how you solved it.

19) What constructive criticism have former bosses made to you, and what did you do in response?

20) If you were hiring for this position, what would you look for?

21) Are you interviewing with other companies?

There are many "right" answers to those questions, and undoubtedly, there are just as many wrong ones. Before reading further, decide what your answers would be. If you have access to a tape or video recorder, record your answers now, and then review your performance. After you have read my suggested responses and reviewed your answers, repeat this exercise.

THE MOST FREQUENTLY ASKED INTERVIEW QUESTION IS

"Tell me about yourself."

What will you say?

Your answer should be no more than two minutes, and yet it will set the tenor for the remaining part of the interview. Plan your reply well in advance and rehearse it often. If you wait until you're sitting in front of the interviewer to come up with an answer, you have blown the interview!

Here are some guidelines:
- Be concise, and keep your response to a maximum of two minutes.
- Be upbeat, emphasizing accomplishments and achievements.
- Include data you want to discuss further during the interview.

Here are some reasons behind the questions and some suggestions for your consideration:

1) *How did you choose your college? Why did you choose your major? What did you intend to do with that degree?*

Even if you attended the University of Saint Playboy-in-the-Caribbean and majored in underwater basket-weaving, you must present a logical reason for doing so. Companies want to feel that you are and have been in control of your life, and that you made your decisions based on a logical career plan.

2) *Why did you leave your past employers?*

Never say anything derogatory about former employers. Rather, you left your previous employment for more responsibility, a greater challenge and a better career opportunity. If your departure was the result of a reduction-in-force, make that clear, and note that your position was not refilled.

3) *Pick three adjectives to describe yourself.*

This must be the oldest and simplest question of all, but it still amazes me how many applicants are stunned when I ask it. There are other ways of phrasing this question, such as "What are your strong points?" or "How would your best friend (or employer) describe you?"

Remember, this is a business interview, so pick adjectives that are business-oriented. Unless you are pursuing a career in the Scouts, do not be "loyal, thrifty, brave, obedient, etc." Here are some good choices: aggressive, ambitious, assertive, self-motivated, goal-oriented, self-disciplined, persistent, good communicator, competitive, team player, etc. Having chosen your adjectives, now think of specific instances illustrating how you have used those qualities, and be prepared to relate them.

4) *Give me a specific example of a problem you overcame in your job.*

The interviewer is essentially asking you what you have accomplished in your job. Choose an achievement that best illustrates your results-orientation.

5) *What are the qualities of a good manager [salesperson, accountant, engineer, etc.]?*

Obviously, you must exemplify the same qualities of a good whatever, so pick adjectives similar to the ones you chose in question #3. Then be prepared with several good illustrations.

6) *How would you rate your success with your job? Why were you successful?*

Always rate yourself highly, but not perfect. Even if you were fired from your last job, you should rate yourself well. On a scale of one to ten, you should pick eight or nine. Why were you successful? Because you possess the qualities of a good whatever that you identified in questions #3 and #5. Again, be prepared with specific examples.

7) *What did you like [or dislike] most about your last job? If you could change anything about your last job, what would it be?*

Since you knew what your job would be, there must have been something about it that you liked, or why else would you have taken it? Thus, you should have many items about your job that you like and only a few that you dislike, although these dislikes obviously outweigh the positive aspects of your job. Above all, do not blame your displeasure on any person, especially your supervisor; the interviewer will question your version of the conflict. Never make any references to location, personality conflicts, or any answer that would allow the interviewer to conclude that you could be the problem.

Let me stress, however, that you should not suppress your feelings about your present employment. If you are seriously considering a job change, then you must have serious misgivings about your job. You should discuss them tactfully, yet frankly and forcefully, showing that you have given this considerable thought and have concluded that your talents would be best used elsewhere. Your thoughts here must be organized and logical, and expressed well enough to convince the interviewer.

8) *Rank these in order of preference: salary, location, nature of the job.*

This is another easy question, but frequently missed. Always have location last, even if you really don't mean it. Should the location of the job be highly desirable to you, don't mention it during your interview. Companies need to think you are more interested in them and their position than you are in where you are located, and thus, nature of the job should be first, except possibly in the case of commissioned salespersons.

9) *Where do you expect to be in your career in five years?*

This can be tough if you don't know the company's normal career path. Certainly you expect to have been promoted, perhaps more than once. I suggest you answer with a question such as, "I expect to have achieved at least one promotion, but I am not familiar with your company's career path for this position. What should I reasonably expect?" Do not give the impression that you expect too much too soon and might become a disgruntled employee. And don't say you expect to be in the interviewer's position; that weak answer went out years ago!

10) *Tell me about yourself.*

Remember the "30-second resume"? Roll it out again, and keep it upbeat and spontaneous. Now you have time to add some more information, especially accomplishments, but keep it to a maximum of two minutes. You know you will encounter this question during nearly every interview, so you should have prepared and rehearsed it well in advance. There is no excuse for not being prepared for this old question.

11) *What do you consider the major accomplishment(s) or achievement(s) in your life and career?*

Surely you must have thought about this many times, but I am always surprised at how often an applicant falls apart when this is asked. Here is your chance to really pat yourself on the back, and don't be shy!

12) *Give me an example of an unpopular policy you had to implement and how you did it.*

This question was recently asked to one of my applicants applying for a personnel management position, and it could also be asked of many other positions. For example, if you are a salesperson, how do you tell your clients about an expected price increase? How do manufacturing managers explain increased productivity goals? Your answer will reveal much about your intelligence, results-orientation, and sensitivity, so be prepared with a thoughtful answer.

13) *Why are you considering a job change?*

Your answer here will be similar to your response in question #2. Now, however, you will add current considerations such as these:

• you are seeking a more dynamic or aggressive company;

• you want to use your knowledge and experience to transfer into a faster-growing industry (avoid saying a more stable industry, which sounds as if you are running away);

• you are seeking a company that will allow you more personal input into daily operations;

• you are seeking a company that gives more personal responsibility for final results;

• you would like to be better compensated for your contribution (especially good for salespersons);

• you would like to be more challenged than you are in your current position.

Note that these answers are positive in tone (versus, "I am *not* being adequately compensated....," etc.) Again, do not denigrate an employer, past or present.

14) *Evaluate your present and past supervisors. (Recent grads may be asked to evaluate their instructors.)*

Here you are displaying your tough-mindedness and objectivity. Using specific examples, mention a few good and bad points about current or former bosses, and how you might have acted differently. Most of your supervisors were probably good, so be certain that your praise is greater than your fault-finding, lest you be considered too negative or possessing a "bad attitude." Also, do not be too derogatory and never personal – you are commenting on performance as a supervisor, not as a "person."

15) *Why haven't you found a job after so many months?*

The standard reply is this: "Finding a job is easy; finding the right job takes a while longer." Quite likely, this will not satisfy the interviewer, and you may be asked for more details regarding your prolonged job search. Since this is essentially a negative discussion, try to end it as soon as possible, without getting defensive. If you have received job offers that you declined, explain why – with good, logical reasons, of course!

16) *What interests you about this job?*

If you don't have a good answer to this question, your interview is over. Your preparation should have given you at least some information about the job, and you must show how your qualities match the nature of this job.

17) *What can you contribute to our organization?*

If you can't sell yourself now, you never will. From your preparation, you should already know how your background and experience will benefit them, so tell them now – be assertive and lay it on thick! Show how their needs mesh closely with your own qualities, and include several examples.

18) *How well do you communicate with others? Give me an example of a communications problem you encountered and how you solved it.*

Over the years, I have reviewed thousands of job requisition forms, and nearly all have listed good communicative skills as a requirement for the job. Spend some time reflecting on how well you communicate your thoughts and ideas, and have several examples ready that demonstrate your ability to overcome problems communicating with others (superiors, subordinates, peers, clients, etc.).

19) *What constructive criticism have former bosses made to you, and what did you do in response?*

In other words, how well do you take criticism? This question is a variation of "What are your weak points?" or "What are your limitations?"

If your answer is that you never have been criticized, then I think you are lying and so will the interviewer! Since we are all imperfect, we all have made mistakes and thus encountered criticism. You must freely and openly admit your shortcomings (but not too many and not too severe!) and give specific examples of what you have done to overcome them.

20) *If you were hiring for this position, what would you look for?*

This is too easy. Describe yourself, using a variation of the adjectives you used in questions #3 and #6.

21) *Are you interviewing with other companies?*

Suppress the urge to answer, "None of your business," even though that may be the case. Reply something like this: "Yes, and it is very important that I choose a position that I will both enjoy and find challenging, as well as a company where I feel comfortable and can establish my career. I would like this job search to be my last. I feel that what ABC Company has to offer is exactly what I am seeking, and I would like to be a part of your organization."

Some interviewers may ask for what positions or with what companies you are interviewing, to determine if you have established a solid job focus. Politely decline to reveal the name of any company, but you can reveal other positions for which you are interviewing, being certain that these positions are similar to the one for which you are being interviewed and thereby confirm your job focus.

These 21 questions and answers are only a few of the many you might encounter, and I do recommend that you write down as many questions and your answers as you can. Then rehearse your answers aloud, perhaps to a friend for criticism.

Relocation

In addition to the above questions, you will undoubtedly be asked about your availability for relocation. How you handle the following questions can determine the result of your interview:

- Are you available for immediate relocation?

- Will you be open for relocation at a later date?

- Does your spouse also have a career, and will relocation be a problem for him/her?[1]

- Are there any potential problems that could affect your relocation, now or in the future?

These are definitely some of the most important questions you will encounter during the interview. I know I may get redundant here, but I must emphasize the importance of how you handle this series of questions. It is paramount that the interviewer feel that your major concern is the job – its nature, responsibilities, scope and potential. Be careful that you say nothing that will give the interviewer the impression that location is more important, or even equally so. If you say anything that leads the interviewer to conclude that location will be a primary factor in your career, you likely will not be considered further.

Unless the company with whom you are interviewing has operations in only one location, you may be required to move to another locale, either now or later. Since restricting your geographic availability eliminates an infinite number of jobs for which you could be qualified, I strongly urge you to consider any relocation as just another part of the total package, and evaluate it accordingly. If you are happy with your job, you most likely will be happy regardless of the location. Plus, companies need to think you are promotable, which usually involves a

---

[1]Yes, this question is legal, although it must be carefully presented so it will not suggest sex discrimination. Usually, it will not be asked so straight-forwardly, but the information somehow will be gleaned.

transfer. If you are just starting your career, you may want to consider other Sunbelt locations, planning to request a transfer or promotion to the Triangle or Triad area when one occurs. In fact, if you really like the company and its career path, that plan is a very viable alternative, especially if your company is headquartered here.

On the initial, screening interview, companies sometimes decline to reveal the location of their opening, in order to determine your promotability/transferability. I have even had companies describe the position as requiring a relocation, even though it was for this area! Furthermore, even if (or especially if) you know the position for which you are interviewing is in your preferred location, you should state your availability for relocation, so that the company will feel you are promotable.

Consequently, unless there are absolutely no circumstances under which you will consider relocation, I urge you to state that you are totally open for relocation, now as well as later. Should you receive a job offer in a location unacceptable to you, you can simply say no. But you will never have the opportunity to evaluate the whole offer, if your restrictions stop the interview process at the beginning.

Realistically, however, I realize that you may have a logical reason for your relocation restrictions, or even simply that you prefer to remain in this area; after all, that is probably why you bought *Raleigh-Durham Jobs*, and not Cleveland Jobs! From my own personnel experiences, I know that finding applicants who will relocate is perhaps the single greatest problem in job placement, and I suggest that most corporate recruiters would concur.

So if you don't want to relocate, how do you answer these questions? That depends on your reasons and how well you present them, although any reason will be viewed with suspicion.

A few years ago, I secured employment in Atlanta for an applicant whose child was undergoing extensive therapy at Emory University Hospital, and thus he needed to remain in Atlanta for the near future. That was an understandable reason, and the company wanted him enough to accept this, at least temporarily.

On the other hand, I also have interviewed hundreds, maybe thousands, of applicants (especially recent grads) who simply liked a specific location, and would not relocate. From a corporate standpoint, that's not a good reason, and again I urge you to reconsider, or at least come up with a better, more acceptable reason.

In between these two extremes are many valid cases for remaining in a specific locale. For example, dual-career families especially can be a potential problem. In this case, tell the interviewer that relocation would be considered, assuming that your spouse could continue his/her career at that locale. In fact, with the rapid increase of two-career families, many companies now offer all sorts of job placement and assistance to relocated spouses, and it would be proper to ask the interviewer if that company has any such programs.

Financial considerations, such as owning real estate here, may seem like a valid reason to you, but from a company's viewpoint, it is merely another roadblock to promotions and transfers. Wanting to be near aging or ailing parents could be acceptable for a short time, but the interviewer will want to know how you plan to handle this situation in the future. If you have still other reasons for wanting to stay here, first try to view them from the company's perspective before you explain them to the interviewer.

In summary, you should be as flexible in your inflexibility as possible. Nevertheless, if there are legitimate reasons for your inability to move, let the interviewer know. Realize, however, that he/she may not agree that your reasons are justified for spurning their career opportunity, and so for the last time, I again suggest you carefully consider your stance on this subject. But whatever you decide, decide it *before* the interview, and be prepared with your answer.

Salary Questions[1]

One of the hardest questions to handle during an interview is "What are your salary requirements?" It is difficult to answer for several reasons:

- You may not know the full scope of the position.

- You are afraid to over-price yourself and miss out on a good career opportunity.

---

[1] For a thorough discussion of salary negotiating, see Chapter VII. For now, we will concern ourselves with the interview questions related to salary.

• If you name a figure too low, that may be interpreted as being under qualified.

• You suspect that your past compensation is higher than they have budgeted for this position and you fear being labeled overqualified.

• You certainly do not want to name a figure that may be less than the salary they are prepared to offer.

In short, if you name a figure too high or too low, you may be eliminated from consideration.

When this question is asked on your first, exploring interview, you have good reason for avoiding an answer, especially if you have not yet determined the full responsibilities and duties of the position. In this case, I suggest you say, "I have researched your company and know that you offer fair and competitive salaries. But since I do not yet know the full scope of the position or its potential, I am hesitant to state a figure now. Can we discuss salary later?" If the interviewer persists, I suggest you give a broad salary range (but not too broad!), adding that you will be able to give a more specific figure when you learn more about the position.

However, if your interview has been arranged through a third party (*e.g.*, a personnel agency or employee of the company), you already should know their salary structure. In this case, omit the run-around and simply say what they want to hear.

After you have had one or more interviews, you should be knowledgeable enough to determine what salary to request. By then, you will know what is expected in the position and you may have been given a hint as to what salary they have in mind. Although you must be prepared to name a salary if pressed, I encourage you to allow the company to state a figure first. If the figure is what you had anticipated, say that the salary is in line with your thoughts too. If the figure is higher than you expected, don't salivate, but simply say that the figure is acceptable.

If the salary stated is less than what you feel the position should command or less than you feel you deserve, then be prepared to negotiate, using the guidelines and principles explained in "Chapter VII: Salary Negotiating."

"Why were you fired?"

Even more difficult to handle are questions concerning your dismissal from a prior job, especially your most recent. Short of an absolute lie, avoid any comment that would reveal that to be the case. Say that you left your position to pursue other opportunities (which is true) and that you have letters of recommendation, should your interviewer wish to see them.[1] However, if you were the victim of a corporate reduction-in-force, state that as the cause and then indicate that your position was not refilled.

Nevertheless, if your interviewer knows you were fired or is perceptive enough to conclude that, be prepared with a counter-attack. Recognize that no excuse will be entirely adequate, but attempt to put your dismissal in the most positive light possible.

The best approach is to be open and honest, and go for empathy. We all make mistakes in life and the important thing is to learn from them. How many times have you heard, "Experience is the best teacher"? Reveal the reason for your termination, and then discuss what you have learned from the experience and what you have done to remedy that situation. Since it is unlikely that you can convince the interviewer that you were fired without cause, you can use your understanding of the firing to show that you have grown professionally, improved your skills, and are now a more valuable employee than before. If possible, have letters of recommendation from previous supervisors that indicate you have performed well in the past.

Personality conflicts are a frequent cause for firing, but I suggest you not blame that, since there are two sides to every issue and the

---

[1] Regarding letters of recommendation, you should always ask for one whenever you change jobs. On future job interviews, you may need one but not be able to locate previous supervisors, who may have changed jobs or moved. Thus, whenever you leave a job, even summer jobs or internships, obtain these letters and keep them on file for future need.

Personnel departments will never authorize a letter of recommendation, for legal reasons too involved to discuss here. However, you often can obtain one from a supervisor. If you were fired by your most recent manager, ask a former supervisor. If you cannot get anyone within your company to write one, then try clients or some other person with whom you dealt in your job. If you have documentation, such as sales quotas or other data that indicate your success, then you can use that instead of a recommendation.

interviewer has no reason to believe your version. Definitely don't imply that for some reason your boss "was out to get you." Instead, consider saying that you had concluded some time ago that your position was no longer challenging and that you were not growing professionally. You had decided to look elsewhere, and your attitude may have reflected that. Then detail your logic in deciding to change jobs. Again, have letters of recommendation to show your success.

Oftentimes, when your company learns that you are actively seeking other employment, you will be terminated immediately. If that was the case, you have an okay excuse available, but you will need to explain why you had decided to leave your employer.

If there was some other reason for your dismissal and you want to discuss it, be certain you have sufficient documentation to support your case.

If you were terminated for immorality or dishonesty, you are in deep trouble, and no excuse is acceptable. Admit your mistake and explain what you have done to overcome it or compensate for it.

Have questions of your own.

Either during and/or at the end of your interview, you must have several pertinent, well-conceived questions to ask. If you don't, the interviewer will think you disinterested or unintelligent; surely everything was not explained thoroughly!

There are some questions you can plan in advance to ask, but you also need to have some spontaneous questions that show you have listened and comprehended what the interviewer has said. Choose questions that show interest in the job, company and career path. Although it is important to ask questions, it is more important to ask *good* questions! And make them flow logically and spontaneously, and not sound rehearsed or "canned."

Here are some suggestions, and you will want to add more:

1) What are the projections for the growth of your company and its industry?

2) What is a reasonable career path for me to expect?

161

3) Why is the position open?

4) What characteristics seem to be present in your most successful employees?

5) Why has your company been so successful?

6) What problems has the company encountered in the manufacturing process [or sales, accounting, engineering, etc.]?

7) What do you want done differently by the next person to fill this job?

Unless specifically asked, here are some topics you should not discuss on your first interview:

1) Salary and benefits. Again, you should seem more interested in the job and potential with the company, than you are in immediate compensation.

2) Location, unless you can work it into the conversation without giving the impression that location is of primary importance.

3) How soon to the first promotion or salary review. Although the interviewer undoubtedly will be evaluating your long-term potential, you must not seem overly concerned with the next step. Rather stress how well you can accomplish the job for which you are interviewing.

Preparation is undoubtedly the most important factor in interviewing, but there are other subjects you should consider. Many of these are "givens," but let's go over them anyway.

1) **Proper dress**: Always dress conservatively and traditionally. Pay attention to details such as polished shoes, clean fingernails, limited cologne, etc. Do not wear anything distracting, such as tinted glasses (I once had an applicant rejected for that) or flashy jewelry. There is no excuse for failing an interview because you were inappropriately attired.

2) **Punctuality**: Always arrive a few minutes early, but never more than ten minutes. If you are not familiar with the area where the interview is to take place, make a practice trip the day or night

before. As with proper dress, there is no excuse for failing the interview because you were late.

3) **Body language**: Sit up straight in the chair and do not slouch. Gesticulate some, but don't get carried away. Be appropriately animated and seem genuinely interested. Project a positive, optimistic mien.

4) **First impression**: Strive to make an excellent first impression. From my own perspective and from my discussion with other interviewers, a truism to remember is that 90% of the interview occurs in the first minute! Offer a firm, dry handshake, and do not sit until told to do so. Be poised, and with an air of self-confidence. Thank the interviewer for seeing you, and then wait for the session to begin.

5) **Ending the interview**: When you sense the interview is over, again thank the interviewer for his/her time and consideration, and shake hands as you leave. If you have not already been informed of their selection process, now is the time to ask. How many additional interviews will be required, and with whom? Ask when you can expect to hear from them, should you be selected for the position.

6) **Thank-you note**: As soon after the interview as possible, send the interviewer a short note expressing your interest and again thanking him/her. Refer to "Chapter VIII: Correspondence" for more information on this subject.

And finally, consider these few admonitions:

1) Never chew gum and do not smoke, even if offered. If having a luncheon or dinner interview, do not drink alcohol.

2) Never use profanity. Over the years, I have been amazed at the number of applicants who were rejected because of this. Even the mildest "four-letter word" could be offensive to the interviewer or may be interpreted as a lack of sensitivity on your part.

3) Never "bad-mouth" former employers or teachers. Present a positive attitude and avoid making any negative statements.

4) Don't make excuses for failures or mistakes. Avoid even mentioning them at all, but if you must, present them as positive learning experiences from which you gained much insight and knowledge.

5) Be careful not to make statements that interviewers might view as "red flags." Try to imagine yourself on the other side of the desk, listening to your answers. Are you saying things that seem to disturb the interviewer? For example, I recently spoke with a former school teacher who was telling potential employers that she resigned from teaching on the advice of her psychiatrist! Almost a year later, she couldn't understand why she hadn't found a job.

Evaluate your interview. Immediately after each interview, sit down with pen and paper, and think through the interview and your performance. Record specific questions you were asked and what a better answer from you might have been. List things you might have done better and how. What did you do well? What did you say that the interviewer seemed to like? Dislike? What have you learned from the interview that will be helpful in future interviews? *This critical evaluation is extremely important; don't skip over it!*

Conclusion

Interviewing – and interviewing well – is a job in itself, and the more you do it, the better you will become. I mentioned earlier practicing with a friend, and I suggest it again. Although some interviewers may not appreciate this, I also suggest that you accept one or two interviews in which you have little interest, just for the interviewing experience.

During the past twenty years, I have interviewed thousands of applicants and overseen the interviews of countless others. In addition, I have discussed interviewing techniques with numerous corporate recruiters and compiled their thoughts also. Thus, the information I have relayed here is from personal knowledge and experience. I guarantee that if you follow my suggestions, you will have the best possible interview.

INTERVIEW CHECK LIST

Have you . . .

√ Researched the company and the position?

√ Rehearsed probable questions and your answers?

√ Prepared your questions?

√ Checked your attire?

√ Packed your resume, business cards, etc.?

√ Determined the location of the interview?

CHAPTER VI

STEP FIVE:

FOLLOW THROUGH

CHAPTER VI

Step Five: Follow Through

Pat yourself on the back; you deserve it! When you reflect on all the work you have done to get to this stage, I'm sure you feel the same.

But don't let up now! There are still a few points to cover, and these are also important in obtaining a job offer.

First of all, a thank-you note[1] is now in order. As soon after the interview as possible, send a short note to express your interest and to thank the interviewer(s) for spending time with you. If you can enclose an item relevant to your discussion, such as a newspaper or magazine article, or can mention some other recent media report, do so. If you are sending more than one note, personalize each with a comment relating to your interview with that person. Most importantly, keep this note short. You have made a good impression; don't ruin it now with overkill.

If you really want this job and definitely are qualified, then consider this: Are there any individuals (former employers or supervisors, clients, college professors, etc.) who would attest to your abilities? If so, ask one or two of them to call the company and give you a verbal recommendation. Should that person also be regarded highly by your potential employer, this well could be the boost that takes you over the

---

[1] See "Chapter VIII: Correspondence" for instructions on writing this note, and to Appendix B for examples.

top. Of course, you cannot use this push after every interview or you will wear out your references. Save it for the special ones you truly want.

The Interview Process

Most companies do not extend job offers after the first interview, unless that interview was an all-inclusive interview with several authorities. Generally, companies have a three-interview process, although this can vary widely from company to company. My personal opinion is that any company that can't make a decision within three meetings has a serious decision-making problem! However, there are companies that will drag out the interviewing and hiring process, so don't be upset if you're called for more interviews.

The first interview is a basic screening, usually conducted by a personnel representative, and this sometimes could be simply a phone interview. The second interview is most often with the primary decision-maker(s) or the person to whom the position will report. By the time you are invited back for a third interview, the decision has been made to offer you the job, or almost so. The final interviewer will be a higher authority, perhaps in corporate headquarters or at the location where you will be employed.

Sometimes the second or third interview will be a simulated role playing or a sort of on-the-job situation. For example, sales applicants are frequently sent to conduct sales calls with a company sales representative. This allows the applicant to better understand the nature of the job and the company's salesperson to relay impressions of the applicant to the hiring authorities.

My reason for explaining the standard procedure is this: If you anticipate that you will be called for another interview, you must do additional research on the company before that next interview. The company will expect that if you are sincerely interested in the position, you will have done something more to learn more about them and/or their position. For example, if you are interviewing for a job in college textbook sales, you could call on a few college professors and ask about the company's books and reputation. If you are interviewing for a position as Plant Engineer, you could do research on the product they manufacture and the process involved, and have several relevant statements and questions ready to show for your efforts.

I cannot overstress the importance of this additional preparation. In practice, I have had applicants rejected after the second interview because they had not taken the time to investigate the company and position further, and thus could not display additional knowledge of the company or its products. Do this extra research; it will separate you from other applicants and impress the interviewers.

CHAPTER VII

SALARY NEGOTIATION

CHAPTER VII

Salary Negotiation[1]

How much are you worth?

You have a job offer, or expect one very soon, and you are concerned about the total compensation package – salary and benefits. Is it enough, and what is "enough"? Could you negotiate a better package?

Many job seekers have developed an attitude that salary negotiation is somehow a "dirty business" and they think that companies frown on any suggestion that you may feel that their offer is inadequate or could be enhanced. This simply is not true, and you need to orient yourself to understand that salary negotiation is just another part of the employment process.

Salary negotiation is not a true science, in that there are no hard-and-fast rules that fit every instance. All negotiating, including salary negotiating, involves some "gut feeling." Even acknowledging that some guesswork and being-in-the-right-place-at-the-right-time is involved, however, the key to "naming your salary" is knowledge:

---

[1] How to answer salary related interview questions, such as "What are your salary requirements?" are discussed in "Chapter V: Interviewing Techniques."

- knowledge of the company's compensation system and its flexibility,

- and knowledge of your ability to perform the job and your value to the company.

Compensation Systems

The first item you need to learn is how the company's compensation plan works. Is it a well-defined system or determined at the whim of the company's owner? During subsequent interviews, but never your first, you can ask questions such as these:

"How is your compensation package determined? Do you have a formal classification system or is it determined on an individual basis?"

"How often do you conduct performance and/or salary reviews?"

Or more to the point, "How are salary, benefits, and promotional opportunities determined with your company?"

Most major corporations, as well as many smaller organizations, utilize a compensation system referred to as a "point-factor system." This means that each job is classified based on several factors, including

1) The requirements needed for the job,

2) The duties and expectations of the job, and

3) The salary range assigned to the position.

These factors will remain constant, regardless of who is in the position. When you are being considered for employment, the interviewer is evaluating you with reference to those three factors, plus one more:

4) How promotable are you? Or, what is your potential with the firm?

Even if the company does not have a formal compensation system, these four factors still will determine your starting compensation, so let's discuss each one.

176

Requirements: If you have the minimum requirements for the job, you can expect the minimum of the salary range. However, if you have additional talents that could be useful later, you can negotiate.

Duties and expectations: How well can you perform the job now and how much training will you need? If you have previous experience doing the same functions or training related to the position, you have a bargaining tool. If you have experience doing the same functions plus additional duties as well, you have another tool.

Salary range: Note that the salary is a salary *range*, not a specific figure. Companies generally prefer to hire at the middle of the salary range ("mid-range") or lower, and reserve the upper range for salary raises to incumbents. However, if you can demonstrate your ability to perform the full job right away, you may be able to go above mid-range.

Long-range potential: No company is so short-sighted that it plans only for its immediate needs. In fact, I have had many applicants rejected for a position for which they were perfectly qualified, but the company determined that they were "not promotable," *i.e.*, they lacked potential for growth within the company. On the positive side, if the company views you as having the ability to thrive in their culture, they may be willing to pay more now.

Now you must answer the question I posed earlier, "How much are you worth"? Several publications list the salaries of many job classifications, and if you are unsure of the salaries being paid to other workers at your level, you can research the information. The libraries in the Triangle and Triad cities and counties have these:

- *Occupational Outlook Handbook*
  (Mostly entry level positions)
  Published by US Government Office, Washington, DC

- *The American Almanac of Jobs and Salaries*
  by John W. Wright
  Avon Books, NYC

The US Department of Labor also publishes salary information that is updated every few years. To order by phone and charge to a major credit card, call the Publications Office in Atlanta at (404) 347-1900 and request the booklet "White Collar Pay - Private Goods Producing Industries."

Since salaries often vary by geographic location, these national figures do not always reflect salaries in the Carolina's. Professional associations frequently conduct salary studies for their specific membership, and if you are a member of an association, you can obtain the information from the headquarters office.

In addition, you can network for the basic information. Call someone in a similar position and ask what the usual salary range is for that position. Ask the personnel agency recruiter with whom you are working. College professors in your field are likely to know the current wage.

Learning about comparable salaries for the position is useful, but you still haven't determined *your* value for this specific situation. By the time you receive the offer, you should know all the duties of the job, as well as your potential with the company. Be as objective as possible, and determine what salary you should expect. You should conduct this self-evaluation before your final interview, if possible, so you will be in the position of knowing whether or not to accept the offer. If you are satisfied that the offer is fair, accept it, and confirm a starting date.

But if you feel you are worth more, then let's negotiate!

Your first effort should be simply to get the salary increased. Tactfully, say that you appreciate the offer and are enthusiastic at the prospects of joining their firm. However, you feel you are worth more than their offer and then explain your reasons. For example, describe the success in your previous employment, stressing your accomplishments and achievements. Or point out that you need no additional training for the position and can be a productive employee immediately.

If the company states flatly that the salary is not negotiable, consider some other possibilities:

Creating a new job classification: One method of negotiating a higher compensation is to create a new position, tailor-made for your background and thus not yet firmly classified. For example, if your previous experience included all the duties for which you are being hired, plus you have some additional experience you also can perform now, you can create a new position above the one for which you are being hired.

Indirect compensation: Another area for negotiation is in "indirect compensation," *i.e.*, benefits and other non-salary considerations. For example, the company may offer to pay for additional education and training courses or they may pay for association dues or you may be able to get another week's paid vacation. An increase in expense allowances or offering the use of a company car are other examples.

Sign-on bonus or executive bonus: These bonuses are one-time cash payments, generally paid when you begin employment. They are not included in your annual salary and do not affect future compensation. Their primary use is in overcoming "internal equity," *i.e.*, paying you more than other employees in the same job classification, but they also can be used simply as an inducement to have you accept the position. This form of additional compensation is becoming more popular, but it is generally reserved for upper level positions.

Performance review: During your interviewing, you should have asked how often the company conducts "performance reviews," a critique of your performance and success in the job. These reviews are generally tied to salary increases, and if the company agrees to review you earlier than usual, you can have your salary increased sooner.

If their offer is not negotiable in any way, then you must decide if you feel the job satisfaction, potential, or some other factors are worth the lesser salary. Continue to be polite and upbeat, and leave on a positive note. Thank the interviewer for the offer and then say that you want to discuss it with your spouse or other family member or friend. State that you will give them a decision by the end of the week or some other specific date; don't say "in a few days or so." Having said that you will call by a certain date with your decision, definitely do so.

Conclusion

We have dealt with the question "What are you worth?" Now I want to make a distinction between that question and "What can you get?"

If you are a consummate negotiator, you might be able to receive an offer that exceeds your worth. Don't do it. You must realize that if you somehow are able to negotiate a compensation higher than what you are worth, you are heading for trouble. When the company realizes your limitations, your career there will be dead. If the offer is fair, don't tamper with it. Save your negotiating skills for a later time when you really need them.

Also, to avoid later misunderstanding, request a letter from your new employer outlining your full compensation agreement (including salary, incentive program, expenses, or any other monetary considerations), starting date, and job title or function. This is a reasonable and accepted request, and I require all of my placements to have this letter prior to beginning employment. Most large corporations provide such a letter as a matter of course, but if it has not been mentioned, you should ask for one. Certainly, never resign your current position without it.

CHAPTER VIII

CORRESPONDENCE

**Cover Letter
Broadcast Letter
Thank-You Note
Salary History**

CHAPTER VIII

Correspondence

COVER LETTER

Think back to our discussion of resume preparation. Remember that the purpose of a resume is to get you an interview and that it must be perfect since it is to be the first impression that the company will have of you. The same is true of cover letters, and more:

- It will be read before your resume, and thus it establishes an even earlier impression of you than does your resume.

- Companies realize that you may have had your resume professionally prepared, and thus the cover letter could be a more accurate reflection of you than your resume.

- It serves as an introduction to your resume, an enticement to the reader to peruse your resume.

- It includes information not on your resume, but requested by the company, such as salary history, restrictions, and availability.

- It can zero in on specific experience you have that fits the needs of the company.

- It allows you to emphasize the accomplishments and achievements that illustrate your general qualifications.

It can also highlight information contained in your resume that is important and germane to the job for which you are applying. However, the purpose of the cover letter is *not* to repeat the same information in your resume. That is not necessary, since your cover letter will always be accompanied by your resume. Rather, you should emphasize factors you feel will be important to the reader and will encourage him/her to read your resume and invite you for an interview. Appendix B contains many examples.

Even still, that is a lot of information to include in one document! Unfortunately, the temptation to expound on every facet of your background can sometimes be overwhelming, and I have received cover letters that were even longer than the accompanying resume!

Thus, *Rule #1* in writing a cover letter is this: Keep it brief and to the point. In my discussions with other personnel managers, I find total agreement in that a short, concise cover letter is more effective than a long, detailed one. Recruiters often feel that a long, wordy letter indicates an excessively verbose person. Don't trap yourself by trying to include too much information.

Rule #2: Strive to make your cover letter appear to be a personal, original response. Your resume is somewhat generic in nature, and the cover letter is your opportunity to make it seem relevant to the company and their needs. Thus, do not adopt an obvious form letter, and never use a fill-in-the-blanks form. If you are sending out a large number of resumes and cover letters, using a word processor can be helpful in personalizing a basic form letter.

Another strong suggestion is to find out the name of the individual with whom you are corresponding, and include it on the envelope and in your letter's salutation. I realize that this is not always possible, but personnel managers really notice which applicants took the extra time to learn their name. It may seem like a minor detail to you, but some recruiters feel it is an indication of thoroughness and attention to detail.

On this subject of originality, let me stress the importance of not copying verbatim a cover letter you have read somewhere, not even the ones illustrated here. I assure you that companies will receive many other copies of it, and your chance to appear original and personal will be lost. To illustrate, there is a popular cover letter now in circulation (its origin unknown to me), which starts with some mumbo-jumbo about being able to set meaningful goals and objectives. I receive at least ten copies of it each week from applicants, each of whom must think that he/she is the only one using it! I recognize it from the first sentence and don't bother to read the rest of it. Not only did it fail miserably to achieve its objective, but it also created somewhat of a negative first impression.

Type your cover letter on the same paper as your resume, and proof-read it carefully for accuracy and neatness. This is the company's initial impression of you, so make it good.

Format

All cover letters have the same basic format, with some variations to suit a specific purpose. The three sections of a cover letter are Purpose, Qualifications, and Closing. Usually these sections are incorporated into three paragraphs, each representing a section. Refer to Appendix B for examples.

1) *Purpose*: The Purpose section explains why you are contacting the company and for what position(s) you would like to be considered. For example, you are responding to a classified ad, you were referred by someone, or you are making a direct inquiry. One or two sentences should be enough for this.

2) *Qualifications*: Although the Qualifications section will be the longest section, it should highlight only the best of your qualifications, not explain in detail. Stress your accomplishments and achievements, and the specific experience or background that qualifies you for your job objective. This section may be one or two paragraphs, depending on your layout, but it should never be more than eight or ten sentences, preferably less. You are trying to make a strong first impression by emphasizing a few hard-hitting facts. If you dilute this with a lengthy description, you will lose the impact.

3) *Closing*: End your cover letter with a standard closing paragraph of two or three sentences. First, thank the reader for his/her time and

consideration. Then state your availability for an interview and indicate that you plan to call in a few days. Do not say you will call to arrange an interview. Although you want your cover letter to be aggressive and upbeat, that is too aggressive and presumptuous, and some recruiters find it offensive.

Now let's address some specific situations:

Responding to Classified Advertising

In this case, your opening Purpose sentence is simply, "I am enclosing my resume in response to your ___(date)___ classified ad for a _____."

Since you have read the ad, you have some knowledge of what the company is seeking. Thus, the objective of your Qualifications section is to show how closely you fit that job description. Refer to the ad, and using your highlighting pen, mark the key factors sought by the company. Then tailor your letter to fit those requirements, using specific references to that ad. You may even use the same words from the ad. One very effective method is to use three or four "bullet sentences" or phrases to emphasize your qualifications that closely match their description.

In addition to the standard information in your closing paragraph, include data not in your resume but requested by the company, such as compensation or availability.

Making a Direct Contact

In the above example, you were responding to a specific opening you knew existed. In making a Direct Contact, you do not have that information, and thus your cover letter will be more open and general.

The Purpose paragraph states that you are writing to inquire about opportunities in your field or job objective. Mention why you chose to contact them (*e.g.*, you read a magazine article about them or you know of their reputation), which makes your letter seem more personal.

The Qualifications section will emphasize a few of your career honors and/or accomplishments. Since you don't know what their needs might be, use this section to show your general patterns of achievement, and don't get too specific.

Close your letter with a standard Closing paragraph.

Referral Letters

In between the response to an ad and a blind Direct Contact letter is this situation. Here, a source you developed through networking has referred you to the company.

In your opening paragraph, mention the person or organization that referred you, and for what position(s). This assumes, of course, that you have permission to use that name and that it will be known to the reader.

The content of the Qualifications section will be dictated by the quantity and quality of information you were given, using a variation of the above two formats. For example, if you were told of a specific opening, use the former; if all you know is that there might be some position, use the latter.

Again, use a standard Closing paragraph.

BROADCAST LETTER

Broadcast letters were discussed in Chapter IV as "Tool #1: Mass Mailings." This correspondence is a one-page information letter, combining the best of the cover letter and resume, and is used in place of a resume with cover letter when you are trying to blanket a large number of companies. Examples are in Appendix A.

Your purpose is to present a few hard-hitting facts about your background that will encourage the reader to call you for more information or a complete resume. Thus, you will include only the most important and positive data, emphasizing what you can contribute to the company's "bottom line."

The most important part of your broadcast letter is the first paragraph, which states your most significant achievement, preferable in only one sentence. This strong opening sentence will gain the reader's attention and serve as an enticement to read further.

Remembering that all companies are very "bottom-line" oriented, you want to direct your appeal to what you can offer the reader and the company. What have you accomplished with your previous employers that contributed ultimately to increased profitability? For example, if you have been in manufacturing management did you increase productivity or decrease rejects? If your background is in human resources, did you find new ways to contain benefit costs or reduce employee turnover? Salespersons should emphasize sales increases or new clients. Select a few of these and include them in your second paragraph.

Next, if you have an advanced degree, special training, and/or other outstanding skills, mention them in a short, separate paragraph. If you don't have advanced education, omit this paragraph. Remember, you are trying to impress the reader with your accomplishments and abilities, not your academics.

Conclude your letter with a vigorous statement such as, "Should you be looking for someone who can bring this expertise to your organization, please call me," or "Should your company be in need of a results-oriented, bottom-line manager, please call me."

In writing your broadcast letter, also follow these guidelines:

- Do not include dates, unless these events happened in the past year.

- Do not specify company names, unless they are recognized as industry leaders.

- Bullet statements are more emphatic than ordinary sentences, but don't overuse them or they will lose their effectiveness.

- This letter must <u>never</u> be more than one page and do not include so much information that the reader loses interest.

THANK-YOU NOTE

You may wonder if this correspondence is really necessary. Frankly, I have spoken with many interviewers who said that they attach little or no significance to these notes, and that the notes will not affect their decision. On the other hand, I have spoken with others who feel that this extra detail is indicative of a more thorough person, one who is willing to do more than may be required in order to assure success.

Even those former interviewers usually admit that it could be the feather that tips the scales, when two applicants are so identically qualified. Since you have nothing to lose and much to gain by sending a short note, I recommend you do so. Several examples are included in Appendix B.

Your reasons for sending a thank-you note are

1) to thank the interviewer for time and consideration,

2) to express your interest in the position, and

3) to reinforce the positive impression you created during your interview.

Remember this is a note, not a letter. It should be only a very few sentences, so do not go into details. Assuming you had a good interview, don't ruin it now with verbosity and overkill. If your interview did not convince the interviewer that you are a likely candidate for the position, now is too late. You should, however, re-emphasize in one or two sentences why you fit the position.

For an additional, personal touch, you can make reference to a topic you discussed during the interview. If you recently read (or heard) a news article you think might be of interest to the interviewer, you can mention it, or better yet, enclose it in your thank-you note.

Thank-you notes can be handwritten for expediency, although type-written is best. As always, proofread carefully for accuracy and neatness. As with cover letters, companies may feel this note is a more accurate reflection of you than your resume.

SALARY HISTORY

I recently surveyed *The News & Observer* Sunday want ads, and observed that at least 90% of the professional-level, company-sponsored ads requested either a salary history, current salary, or salary required. In addition, numerous search firms also have begun asking that information. Some companies even stated that those resumes accompanied by salary histories would be considered first, or that resumes without a salary history would not be considered at all!

For many reasons, you often would rather not reveal your salary information prior to the interview. If your salary or salary requirements are too high or too low, you may be excluded from a job for which you are qualified and that you really want. Perhaps you are willing to accept a salary cut in order to remain in the area, to gain valuable experience, to associate with a more dynamic company or industry, or to change career directions. But for whatever reason, you would like not to include this requested information – but you must. How?

If you are being asked only for current salary or salary required, you can include that in your cover letter, either in the final paragraph or in a separate paragraph. If salary is not your main motivation, you can add that you are more interested in other factors than compensation. Here are some examples, and others are included in Appendix B.

> Thank you for your time and consideration, and I will call you next week to confirm that you have received my resume. My current salary is $45,000, and although I am seeking a comparable salary, I am more interested in long-range potential and opportunity with your company.

> As I am seeking to make a career change from sales into manufacturing management, I do not expect to maintain my current salary of $45,000. Rather, I am more interested in developing my new career, using my product knowledge and experience, and thus the career opportunity with your company is my priority.

However, if salary is a primary consideration, make that clear:

> Thank you for your time and consideration, and I will call you in a few days to confirm that you have received my resume. My current salary is $55,000, and I am seeking compensation in the $60,000 range.

Salary histories can be handled in one of two ways. If you have been employed for only a few years with the same company and have had no major promotions or salary increases, a simple addition to your cover letter is sufficient:

> During my five-year employment with ABC Corporation, I have progressed from a trainee salary of $23,000 to my current base salary of $36,000. In addition, I receive a quarterly incentive

bonus, up to 10% of base salary, and a car and expense account are furnished.

If you have had more than one employer or have received several promotions, you may wish to include a separate "Salary History" page. Examples are given in Appendix B.

Whether you include this information in your cover letter or on a separate sheet, keep in mind why companies want this information. The most obvious reason is to ascertain if your salary requirements are within the salary range they are offering, but there are other, more subtle reasons as well.

You may remember in our interviewing discussion that interviewers evaluate your life patterns – that is, demonstrated patterns of success, accomplishment, over-achievement, etc., and the opposites. If your salary history reflects a steady increase in salary, it suggests success with your company(s). If your salary has been decreasing or vacillating, that suggests problems. Also, if your salary is far below your peer group, it will be viewed negatively. Consequently, if you have some oddity in your salary history, you should explain it in one or two positively-worded sentences.

Conclusion

You may have noticed a recurrent theme running throughout this chapter – and for that matter, throughout the entire book. That theme is to keep all of your correspondence concise, to the point, and relevant to your objective. Trust me on this one: company interviewers and other readers really respect the applicant who can sift out the chaff from the wheat. I am not suggesting that you exclude important information in the name of brevity, but that you learn to discern the important from the unimportant, and the most important from the less important. You need only to include the information necessary for the reader to get an accurate, positive assessment of your skills and abilities. Beyond that, you are wasting your words and the reader's time.

CHAPTER IX

"WHAT AM I DOING WRONG?"

CHAPTER IX

"What am I doing wrong?"

Following my suggestions will yield all the interviews you can handle. Take care not to tire yourself by planning too many interviews in a short period. Interviews can be stressful, and you should plan to have no more than two on one day. Plus, you need time to research each company before the interview.

In today's slow economy, many applicants are finding their job search has stretched into many months, often through no fault of their own. Keeping a positive attitude in light of mounting bills is difficult, and casting blame on the economy, yourself, or some other factor is not helping either.

If you think you are following my plan but still not finding enough interviews, then you need to conduct some serious evaluations of your job search techniques. Conducting an objective evaluation of yourself may be difficult, and you may need to ask others for help. What you see in the mirror could be entirely different from what someone else may see.

Evaluate your organization. Are your materials organized so that you can refer to them quickly? Are you spending enough time on your job search and is your time well planned? Are you keeping complete records of your activities and are you following through on all you have learned?

Evaluate your resume. Have you discussed your resume with any-one, especially a corporate recruiter? Does your resume emphasize accomplishments and achievements? Would a topical resume format be more effective?

From my experiences, the most common resume mistake is having a resume that is too long or detailed. A two-page resume is the most you need, and one page is definitely preferable. If you have reduced the margins or the size of the type to squeeze your information onto two pages, then you have too much.

Lately I have spoken with a number of job seekers who blamed their resume for a lack of interviews. In some cases they were at least partially correct, but generally speaking, the problem was more in their marketing approach than with the resume. Don't waste time nit-picking your resume, when that time would be better spent on your marketing efforts.

Evaluate your marketing approach. First, reread Chapter IV, and I'll bet you have overlooked some of the tools I have described. Are you attending job network groups? Have you used the free services described in the Public Agencies section? Have you sought out privately funded organizations that offer job assistance to specific constituencies (*e.g.*, African-American, women, older employees, etc.), including those I listed? Are you attending professional association meetings? Have you conducted "information interviews"? How effective is your "30-second resume"? You may even need to read this text a third or fourth time, in order to catch every suggestion mentioned.

Are you spending enough time cultivating a job network? Recognizing that more job seekers find employment through some form of job networking than all other methods combined, constantly strive to add new contacts to your networking resources.

Evaluate your interviewing techniques. Have you practiced your interview with a friend? Have you listed potential questions and your answers, and discussed them with someone who will know how to in-terview correctly? Do you objectively evaluate your interview after each one? Have you asked the recruiter at a personnel agency where you are registered to critique your interview? Have you recontacted a company with whom you interviewed to ask their human resources representative for a critique of your interview there? When asking for opinions, stress that you really need an honest, objective answer, and don't become defensive to what you hear.

Videotaping a mock interview could be very helpful in graphically revealing your mistakes, but if that is not possible, you should at least audio-tape your interview for evaluation. Have a friend conduct the interview and test you with questions that you are not expecting.

Evaluate your personal appearance. Individuals often have difficulty judging their own appearance, and family and friends may find this too personal to discuss objectively. I encourage you to ask a non-interested acquaintance or business associate for an unbiased, blunt critique of your over-all appearance, not just your attire. If you have the time and money, there are several listings in the Yellow Pages for "image consultants," but for free advice, you can ask your personnel agent or outplacement counselor. Believe me, companies are very aware of the image you would project as their employee!

Evaluate your product - yourself. Back in Chapter IV, I made the analogy that you are now in a sales/marketing position, with yourself as the product. Just as every company periodically evaluates its product line, you too must objectively appraise your career potential to include the future trends in your industry and your ability to remain competitive in it. In today's rapidly changing world, your industry or specialty may be going the way of the dinosaurs. For example, is your industry growing? Do you have the advanced training or education needed to keep ahead of your peers? Now could be the time to consider a career change or to study the advancements in your field. Also, in choosing which companies to target, lean toward the ones considered to be industry leaders, not the "has-beens."

Evaluate your attitude. I recently read an article suggesting that half of your job search success depends on your attitude and behavior. Are you really trying or have you decided, "What's the use?" Are you projecting an air of desperation? Has your prolonged job search tinged your interviews with bitterness or sarcasm? Keep your interviews upbeat and strive to maintain your self-confidence, even in the face of repeated disappointment.

When your job search has begun to run out of steam, don't panic. Calmly sit down and assess what you have done so far: What has worked best? What has been less successful? Don't be afraid to try new approaches and ideas, especially various forms of job networking.

Energizing Your Marketing Approach

I am often asked what is the most common mistake made by job seekers. Although there are many, probably the worst is a poor marketing approach. Too many applicants conduct a "passive" job search when they should be more "active." Let me illustrate.

Applicants frequently tell me that this is the first time they have had to look for a job themselves, that in the past they received unsolicited calls from companies offering them a job. The implication here is that a job search is somehow beneath them and that they are afraid to get their hands dirty looking for one. I personally don't care if this is their first or tenth job search, but they are embarrassed and uncomfortable with their relative position. This psychological discomfort encourages and allows them to take the easy way out and attempt a "passive job search":

• They call personnel agencies, hoping that these firms will do all the work for them;

• They buy a book with hundreds or thousands of company names and addresses, and then blindly send out as many resumes as they have stamps; or

• They read the want ads and respond to every one that sounds even vaguely close to their background.

And then they sit at home, waiting for the phone to ring with their next glorious job offer. Or they go play tennis, occasionally checking for messages on their answering machine.

True, personnel agencies do find jobs for their applicants; your "resume blizzard" occasionally might locate an opening; and companies obviously will hire from their classified advertising. Nevertheless, remember that fewer than 25% of all job seekers will find their jobs through the total of these three sources combined. If you passively sit waiting by the phone, you still may be sitting there long after your unemployment benefits have expired!

My sarcasm is not meant to further irritate sensitive nerves, but to point out the folly of the "passive job search." You need to be conducting an "active job search," using as many approaches as possible and remaining in control over all the segments in your search:

• Instead of calling all the personnel agencies listed in the Yellow Pages, research which ones will be most helpful to you, using the criteria described in Chapter IV. Then establish a strong working relationship with those few agencies.

• Prudently select the companies to which you send your resume, contacting only those you have reason to think will have recurring needs for your background. Appendix C contains detailed profiles of the most active hiring companies in the Triangle/Triad region, inlcudingthe types of individuals they generally seek. You may need to do additional research as well. Limiting your resume blizzard to those companies will save time and money by not sending your resume to companies who will have no interest. Moreover, you will receive fewer rejection letters!

• In responding to classified ads, follow the procedure outlined in Chapter IV, phoning the companies first when possible and then following up on your resume.

Those steps will cover your bases with the "visible job market," but if you stop there you will be eliminating the other 75% of available job openings. Now you should add these to your job search:

• Remembering that more job seekers find employment through some form of job networking than through all other sources combined, establish a job networking campaign. Use professional associations, job network groups, "information interviews," and other sources that you develop. These tools are discussed fully in "Chapter IV: Get That Interview!"

• Volunteer your time to help at associations, not just your professional group, but other non-profit or charity organizations. Volunteering will allow you to display your abilities to a new set of contacts, many of whom may be executives with useful connections. In addition, you will keep your skills current and have a positive outlet for your frustrations.

• Search out your college alumni association, speak with the president, and plan to attend their meetings. You likely will find alumni with backgrounds and degrees similar to yours, and their experiences can be very helpful in your job search. Also, many alumni associations have a job search coordinator to help members and some conduct annual job fairs.

• Use public agencies to locate government jobs, as well as some private sector jobs. List with public job banks, newsletters, and free computer job matching systems.

• Locate privately funded organizations that offer employment assistance for specific minority groups, as well as other special-need groups. Several of these organizations are mentioned in Chapter IV, and you may find others as well.

• Add helpful publications to your data base, to be used for your marketing campaign and for interview preparation. Visit your public library and review the many publications in their career help section.

• Use personnel agencies for more than just company contacts. A knowledgeable personnel recruiter can make valuable suggestions regarding your resume, interviewing techniques, appearance, and more.

No company can exist for long if it passively relies on the whims of others. On the contrary, companies are actively reviewing their marketing techniques at all times and using as many approaches as possible. You too must aggressively market your product – yourself – as much and in as many ways as possible.

Interviewing Faux Pas

During the past twenty years, I have interviewed thousands of applicants and overseen many of their interviews with companies. Here are the major interviewing mistakes I have observed.

• *Failure to prepare.* You must never attempt an interview without prior research and preparation. If you're nervous before an interview, that could be a sign you are not adequately prepared. Being prepared not only settles the stomach, it impresses the interviewer as well!

Your preparation will include three factors:

1) Research the company (and when possible, the interviewer). Call the company and request an annual report, information brochure, or recruiting information to be mailed to you. Visit your local library or the placement department of a local college and review their company information. Network, by asking friends and business associates what they know of the company.

200

2) Anticipate certain questions from the interviewer. Write down in advance as many probable questions as you can and decide your answers. Start with the most popular interview question of all, "Tell me about yourself."

3) Plan questions of your own. There are some questions you can plan in advance to ask, but you also need to have some spontaneous questions that show you have listened and comprehended what the interviewer has said. Choose questions that show interest in the job, company, and career path.

• *Lack of focus.* This is especially true of recent grads, but older applicants suffer from this also. If I had a dime for every applicant who has expressed a desire for "personnel" or "public relations," I could retire tomorrow! When I then ask why they want a career in personnel, they all answer, "Because I like people." Believe me, simply "liking people" is no logic for pursuing a career in personnel – which incidentally in now called Human Resources anyway – and no interviewer will accept that answer. Worse still is the reply, "I enjoy entertaining," as a reason for a career in public relations.[1]

If you really do want a career in Human Resources, your answer should be more like this: "I have spoken with a number of human resources professionals to learn more about the field. I think that the skills I possess closely match those that seem to be necessary for success in human resources, and I especially feel that my ability to listen carefully and then analyze what I have heard could be developed as a recruiter. In addition, I am interested in learning more about government regulations concerning compensation and benefit programs, and I have recently attended a seminar sponsored by the International Foundation of Employee Benefit Plans." That answer shows a seriousness and commitment, not just a frivolous afterthought, and your interviewer will be impressed.

In short, your reasons for pursuing a specific career objective must be well-defined and expressed with a clear knowledge of why you expect to be successful in that capacity. In other words, you must show job focus.

---

[1] In all fairness, I must confess that when I decided to leave teaching and moved to Atlanta to seek a new career, I listed my two career objectives as "personnel" and "public relations." I have learned a lot since then!

- *Unwillingness to relocate.* Unless you are interviewing with a company that has only one location, you must accept the possibility of relocating to another city at some time in your career with them. In fact, unless you say otherwise, companies will expect you to be available for transfers, especially for a promotion. And if you do indicate your unwillingness to relocate, your interview will be dead at that moment!

I strongly urge you to say that you are open for relocation, even if you would rather not, in order to continue the interviewing process. The offer may be so tempting that you will forget your reluctance to move, or the initial assignment could be just where you want to be. Even if the offer is not what you want, you will never have the chance to evaluate it if you cut off the possibility of an offer early in the interviewing process by saying "no" to relocation.

- *Verbosity*. This is my own personal "pet peeve," and I have seen many applicants flunk an interview because they didn't know when to stop talking. If this is a well-developed character trait of yours, there may be little you can do to curb it now. Try objectively to listen to yourself, and if you are taking more than three or four minutes to answer a simple question, you probably are talking too much. Interviewers are much more impressed with a concise answer than a long, detailed one.

- *Profanity*. I am constantly amazed at the number of applicants who use profanity during an interview, and I have had dozens of applicants rejected for this reason. Even the mildest four-letter expletive may be offensive to your interviewer, and it will be viewed as insensitive and immature.

- *Blaming others for your problems at work, especially a supervisor.* Why should the interviewer accept your version of the situation? Never denigrate an employer or supervisor, or complain that you were mistreated. When asked why you are changing jobs, the best answer is that you are seeking a greater challenge and more opportunity for career advancement.

If you were fired, acknowledge your mistake and explain what you have done to overcome the problem. If your termination was the result of a reduction-in-force, stress that your position has not been refilled.

- *Too much emphasis on salary and benefits.* Never bring up the subject of compensation on your first interview with a company, unless you have firmly established your ability to perform the job and have shown strong interest in the company and position. Generally speaking, wait for the interviewer to broach the subject first.

• *Being overly concerned with promotions*, especially the first promotion. Similar to the problem above, don't give the impression that you are more concerned with your first promotion and/or salary review than you are in performing the position for which you are interviewing. This will be interpreted as a concern that you may become bored with the initial assignment or that you feel over-qualified for the job.

The company indeed will be evaluating you as a career employee, including promotions, and that will be a major factor in their decision to hire you or not. Nevertheless, you want to impress on them your ability to perform the job at hand. During the interviewing process, you may ask what their career path usually entails, but avoid asking directly, "How soon to the first promotion?"

• *Not showing enthusiasm for the job.* Always appear enthusiastic about the job and the company, until you have decided the position is not right for you. Unless you demonstrate your enthusiasm, the interviewer will assume you are not interested and may offer the position to some other candidate. And if you do want the job, don't hesitate to say so, clearly and emphatically!

• *"Applicants say and do the dumbest things."* This catch-all category includes blunders such as these:

• The school teacher who told the company interviewer she was changing careers on the advice of her psychiatrist;

• The young man who freely acknowledged that he was fired for having an affair with his boss's wife (in fact, he seemed pleased!);

• The applicant who supplied a potential employer with personal references who gave him terrible recommendations;

• The recent grad who told interviewers he wanted a job for a year or two, until he decided to begin graduate school.

Every personnel recruiter has a list of these jewels, and we often enjoy sitting around and exchanging laughs over them. Maybe one day I will write a book about them, and also include some of the funniest resumes I have received. You wouldn't believe some of the resumes job applicants send out – ah, but that must wait for another day!

You too may be saying something absurd without realizing it. When evaluating your interviewing techniques, try to imagine yourself on the other side of the desk, listening to your answers. In your analysis of each interview, observe which answers seemed to disturb the interviewer.

Conclusion

This covers most of the mistakes you may be committing, but now it is up to you to make corrections. In your planning, allot time for frequent evaluations and analyses of your job search methods, and how you can improve on them. Use as many approaches as you can, and be open to suggestions for still more.

You probably have heard the truism, "Finding a job is a job in itself." Now you understand what that means.

CHAPTER X

CONCLUSION

CHAPTER X

CONCLUSION

I am often asked for a final word of advice to job seekers, and I generally reply _persistence_. Persistence takes many forms:

• If you have decided that after much thought and logical reasoning, you want a specific job or a specific company and you think you are qualified, don't take "no" for a final answer. Keep trying, using as many techniques as you can for gaining an interview and evaluation, and you may have your wish. I have witnessed many surprises over the years, so be persistent!

• Probably the hardest part of conducting a job search is keeping your spirits up, especially when you have just received a mail box full of rejection letters. Remember "Persistence," say it aloud several times, put the letters away, and then immediately start back to work on your job search.

• As I have said many, many times, networking may be the most time consuming marketing tool, but it always yields the best results. Even though you may be tired of all the networking meetings, continue to attend them. When you would rather do anything than speak with another potential source, call anyway. You never know when the next encounter may be **the** one.

Accepting New Employment

YES! All the organization, preparation, and work has paid off! But before accepting a job offer, evaluate it thoroughly.

If you already have decided to accept or reject the offer, you certainly can say so when the offer is extended. If you have not, however, don't feel pressured into making a decision on the spot. Rather, you should thank the person for the offer, express how highly you value the company and position, and then state that you will give them your decision on a specific date, usually less than a week. Do not say "in a few days," but specify exactly when.

Don't be frightened into accepting the first offer you receive, but don't reject it just because it is the first offer and you wonder what else is available. Sit down with pen and paper and objectively decide if it is best for you. Draw a line down the center of the paper and label one side "pro's" and the other, "con's." Here are some factors to consider, and you may have other priorities as well:
• Salary (Review "Chapter VII: Salary Negotiation," if necessary.)
• Location
• Job responsibilities
• Potential with the company
• Experience to be gained
• Company reputation
• Most importantly, how does this position fit in with your career plans, immediate and long-term? How will it look on your next resume?

Dealing with rejection

Life indeed would be nice if you received an interview from every company you contact and a job offer from every interview. Unfortunately, that is just not reality.

In my discussions with job seekers, I have found that dealing with rejection is a very common problem. Although I am not a psychologist, I do have some observations on the matter, and I can offer some suggestions on coping with it, and even using it to your advantage.

Let's say that you contacted 25 companies, got 23 "no interests," and two interviews. (Actually that's really good. Don't be surprised if it takes 100 calls!) The first interview was so-so, but you felt that the second interview went extremely well, and thus you excitedly are planning to do more research. Then you receive a rejection letter in the mail. Or worse yet, you never hear from them again, and they refuse to return your phone calls. How do you handle it?

All those personalized cover letters, all those phone calls, all that research – none of it paid off! But did it?

Well, for one thing, there are 25 fewer companies for you to contact. Your research taught you where to find company information, and you gained knowledge on an industry.

Better still, there is one more item you may be overlooking: feedback from the interviewer. Once you know you didn't get the job, call the interviewer and very politely inquire why. Were you not qualified or did you present yourself poorly? Does he/she have any suggestions for you? If the interviewer will be honest with you, this information alone is worth all of your efforts.

Occasionally applicants call me back and want to know why I will not refer them to a certain job opening or why they were turned down for a position for which they had interviewed. When I try to explain, they become defensive and argumentative, and so instead of giving them good feedback and advice, I just shut down and try to end the conversation as quickly as possible.

Those applicants missed out on some excellent constructive criticism that could have been very helpful in future interviews. Thus, when asking for this constructive criticism, do not be argumentative, but leave with a positive impression. Stress your need for good critiques and advice. Also, there may be another job opening later that you will fit.

Nevertheless, you must accept the fact that you will hear "No" far more often than you will "Yes." That's life, and we simply learn to expect it and deal with it. During your career search, you will speak with many people – companies, agencies, network sources, *et al.* – but unfortunately, only a few will be able to assist you. Surely they would if they could, and they harbor no personal ill will toward you.

Anticipate the problems and rejections you will undoubtedly encounter, and learn to face them with a positive attitude. When needed, call on your emotional support system for a lift. In addition, allot time to work on developing and maintaining your self-confidence and a strong self-image. Then begin each day with the enthusiasm needed to start over at Step One, if necessary. After all, tomorrow is another day!

Beyond rejection

If you have correctly followed the steps in the **CAREER SEARCH SYSTEM,** you should be receiving interviews and offers. If you are not, then I suggest that you may not have assessed realistically your wants or abilities, and you are interviewing for positions that are not available or that are beyond your grasp.

Perhaps you should consult an industrial psychologist or career counselor to gain insight into your capabilities. Consider taking courses or re-training for one of the "hot" fields of the '90's, such as the environment, health care, or computer science.

The System works! I know it does, because I have seen it in action countless times. Follow it through and you will have a most successful job search.

Best wishes!

FINAL SUGGESTION

After you have accepted new employment, send a thank-you letter to all the people who helped you or even tried to help, letting them know of your new assignment and new responsibilities. You may need their help again in the future, plus they may alert you to other opportunities later.

APPENDIX

A. Sample Resumes, References,
    and Business Cards. . . page 215
B. Sample Correspondence . . . page 233
    • cover letters
    • broadcast letter
    • salary histories
    • thank-you notes
C. Profiles of Selected Companies . . . page 247
D. Personnel Agencies . . . page 275
E. Professional and Trade Associations . . . page 279

APPENDIX A:

SAMPLE RESUMES, REFERENCE PAGES, and BUSINESS CARDS

The following resumes all conform to the CAREER SEARCH SYSTEM principles of the "Power Resume":
- All emphasize accomplishments and achievements when possible.
- They are all very positive in tone and include no negative factors.
- They are neat, accurate and to the point.
- Most are one page, or two pages maximum.
- All were typed with at least an electronic typewriter and letter-quality printer. Most were formatted using a word processor and printed with a laser printer.

I have included examples of several different backgrounds (accountant, engineer, sales rep, etc.), formats (functional/chronological and topical) and various lay-outs. There are also resumes for a career change (named "Tanner" and "Lindsey"), re-entering the workforce ("Rose"), and one illustrating combining jobs ("Smith"). In addition, you will find good examples of the use of "Objective" and/or "Summary" (or sometimes "Qualifications"), the inclusion and omission of "Personal," and various methods of describing your education.

The sample business cards are neat, informative, and uncluttered. They do not attempt to be a condensed resume.

LLANA S. FRANCO

Temporary address:
348 Bulldog Drive
Athens, GA 30601
(404) 353-7621

Permanent Address:
1234 Azalea Road NW
Atlanta, GA 30327
(404) 262-7890

Summary

Recent college graduate majoring in **International Business and Spanish**. Career objective is employment with a multi-national corporation, preferably with operations in Latin America. Areas of interest include marketing, international banking and finance, and import/export operations.

Education

UNIVERSITY OF GEORGIA, Bachelor of Business Administration, graduation planned for June, 1990. Relevant curriculum has included the following:

- Macro and Micro Economics
- Principles of Accounting I & II
- International Marketing
- Statistics
- Commercial Spanish
- Business Law I & II

Employment

IBM Corporation (Summer Internship, 1989):
Diverse duties giving exposure to the operations of a major multi-national corporation. Worked in both Marketing and Personnel departments, under minimal supervision. Operated IBM 5520 Word Processor.

Elson's Gift Shops, Atlanta International Airport (Summers 1986 - 1988):
Sales Clerk, serving international passengers and using Spanish and Portuguese languages daily.

U S Army Hospital, Fort Benning, GA (Summer 1985):
Medical Clerk, working with wounded Salvadoran military personnel.

Personal

Born January 23, 1968 . . . . . Single, excellent health . . . . . Open for travel and relocation, including international . . . . . Fluent in Spanish and Portuguese . . . . . Interests include international events, reading and art.

References available on request.

EDMOND R. SMITH

1200 Franklin Road, Apt. F-1
Charlotte, NC 28754
(704) 847-1234

Summary

College graduate with double major in Accounting and English, and with more than fifteen years financial experience. Consistently promoted as a result of dependable performance culminating in accurate accomplishments. Seeking position as **Internal Auditor** or **Financial Control Supervisor**. Open for travel and relocation.

Experience

AUDITING:

Western Union Telegraph Co. (12/84 - present)
As *Senior Internal Auditor* and *Supervisor Financial Control,* conducted autonomous audits of all accounting and money order processing functions. Detected and corrected error in audit procedure, resulting in a revenue increase of $272,000 per year. As *Internal Audit Supervisor*, reviewed work papers, prepared audit reports and supervised up to eight staff auditors in performance of all internal audit assignments.

PRIVATE ACCOUNTING:

Convenient Systems, Inc. and E. L. Lowie & Co. (9/79 - 11/84)
As *Assistant Controller*, supervised eight accountants in the preparation and adjustment of monthly financial statements. Designed and implemented new profit and loss statement format for retail and manufacturing locations. As *Accounting Manager*, supervised accounting staff of six, and insured proper and accurate recording of all daily accounting transactions.

PUBLIC ACCOUNTING:

A. M. Pullen & Co. (6/76 - 9/79)
As *Senior Accountant,* planned and conducted audit engagements; drafted audit programs; prepared time budgets, financial statements and accountants' reports; and filed federal, state and city tax returns.

Education

University of North Carolina at Greensboro
Accounting major, 1976
Maintained GPA 3.0/4.0

University of North Carolina at Chapel Hill
Bachelor of Arts in English Education, 1973
Financed education through summer employment, student loans and part-time employment during school year.

SUSAN B. SWIFT
3829 Helen Lane
Durham, NC 27702
(919) 282-4837

PROFESSIONAL EXPERIENCE

Professional background has been selling food products to the grocery industry, including twelve years experience as a food manufacturer's representative. Worked with two national manufacturers calling on grocery chains, wholesalers and drug chain accounts, covering the states of Georgia and Florida. Extensive experience with food brokers, headquarters presentations, new item introductions, business reviews, and SAMI and Nelson data.

EMPLOYMENT HISTORY
1987 to present

Wyeth-Ayerst Laboratories, Philadelphia, PA
Sales Manager, Atlanta District
Manage sales, promotions, pricing and plan-o-grams. Full sales responsibility for grocery chains, wholesalers and drug accounts for the sales of infant formula in Georgia and Florida. Sell and coordinate distribution with 51 major accounts with total sales of $6.7M in 1987. Performed under an MBO system for bonuses and pay raises.
Accomplishments:
- 45% sales increase (1989 over 1988)
- 42 new item placements in 1989
- Manage Eckerd Drug Company account
- Manage major food brokerage companies in Georgia and Florida

1985 - 1987

Common Communications, Atlanta, GA
Sales Representative
Calling on large and small business owners, sold communications equipment and systems. Developed clientele through referrals and cold calling.

1977 - 1985

Sunshine Biscuit Company, Atlanta, GA
Account Manager
Supervised and coordinated activities of two major retail chain accounts. Full sales responsibilities, including promotions, business reviews, credits and new item presentations. Also maintained 55 other retail accounts.
Accomplishments:
- 30% sales increase per year for three consecutive years with Kroger account
- 1981 received Salesman of the Year Award for highest division sales

EDUCATION

B. B. A., Georgia State University, Atlanta, GA, 1979.
Self-financed all personal and tuition expenses.

FRANK N. CHRISTOPHER

398 Colony Court
Smyrna, GA 30020
(404) 435-0876

OBJECTIVE	Marketing and sales position with a product- or service-oriented firm, where experience and qualifications can be effectively used. Seeking career opportunity conducive to personal and professional growth.
QUALIFICATIONS	**Background and Scope of Development**: Currently employed as Marketing Representative with Xerox Corporation. Prior experience with IBM Corporation and First Atlanta Bank. Master's Degree and Bachelor's Degree in Business Administration. **Capabilities**: Three years of corporate sales experience has involved such areas as cold calling, prospecting, territory management and extensive sales training.
EXPERIENCE	**XEROX CORPORATION** June 1986 - present *Marketing Representative* • Market entire office product line of computers, typewriters, copiers, facsimile and systems. Activities include developing new accounts and managing established accounts. Accomplishments: Consistently surpass sales quotas and performance goals. **IBM CORPORATION** February 1985 - May 1986 *Marketing Support Intern* • Responsibilities included cold calls, sales and training of IBM equipment for the general sales force. Accomplishments: Achieved highest sales ranking of the year during internship. **FIRST ATLANTA BANK** September 1982 - January 1985 *Financial and Budget Analyst* • Prepared detailed financial data including the assets and liabilities of First Atlanta Bank and holding companies, and presented monthly to senior management.
EDUCATION	Samford University, Birmingham, AL **MASTER OF BUSINESS ADMINISTRATION,** June 1985 **BACHELOR OF SCIENCE** in Marketing, June 1982 Activities: Served as President of Alpha Kappa Psi, business fraternity; Vice-President, Pi Kappa Phi, social fraternity; President, Intrafraternal Council.

LOUIS C. CARTWELL

1234 Apple Lane NW
Columbia, SC 29202
(803) 250-0215

Summary

MBA graduate with five years management experience in United States Army as commissioned officer. Seeking Management Development Program with a major corporation, utilizing well-developed supervisory skills.

Experience

UNITED STATES ARMY
(June 1984 - present)

CAPTAIN, eligible for promotion. Available for employment October 1990. Summary of duties and responsibilities follows:

Maintenance Management: As Company Maintenance Officer, coordinated all scheduled and unscheduled maintenance for organic vehicles, engineer and support equipment from 1985 to date. Managed training of all maintenance personnel and equipment operators to insure cost effective utilization of manpower and material.

General Management: Managed safety program for the 8th Aviation Company in 1986 - 1987. As Safety Officer, identified areas of high accident potential, suggested corrective actions and educated unit personnel in accident proofing techniques. Managed Unit Postal Facility serving eighty men. While Platoon Leader in an aviation unit, motivated and trained up to 25 men in the accomplishment of a wide variety of activities. Served six months as Financial Custodian over funds for 1,000 dependent children.

Aviation: Received private pilot's license in 1984. Completed Army Aviation helicopter training with honors in 1985 and received FAA commercial helicopter certification. Have flown 850 accident-free hours to date flying VIP missions in support of the Division Commanding General and his staff.

Education

MASTER OF SCIENCE in Business Administration with honors, Boston University, 1987. Completed program while working full-time in the Army.

BACHELOR OF BUSINESS ADMINISTRATION in Management, North Georgia College, 1984. Served as President, Student Government Association. Active in Sigma Nu fraternity, distinguished Military Graduate.

Personal

Born November 27, 1963. . . . . 6'0", 170 lb., excellent health. . . . . Married, one child. . . . . Open for travel and relocation. . . . . Interests include historical reading, tennis, racquetball and physical fitness. . . . . References available on request.

CHARLES G. PULLER

244 Mecklenburg Avenue
Greensboro, NC 28664
(919) 954-1042

Objective

To secure a position in Manufacturing Management, either in production, operations or administration, where education, abilities and experience can be best utilized.

Experience

JOHN H. HARLAND COMPANY, printer of bank stationery and other commercial printing. (1981 - Present)

PRODUCTION MANAGER, Greensboro, NC (1986 - present):
Have profit center responsibility for subsidiary involved in technical printing (forms, stationery, cards and mail order checks) and related direct mail operations. Direct the activities of four Supervisors managing a staff of 40 persons. Oversee inventory/quality control, efficiency, personnel, audit preparation and purchasing. Extensive involvement in overall company efficiency planning.
> *Accomplishments*: Reduced labor costs by 5% per month. Boosted profit margin by 4% (from minus 2% to plus 2% level). Won "Best Quality Division" awards (1987 and 1988). Reduced turnover from over 50% to under 20%.

ASSISTANT PLANT MANAGER, Orlando, FL (1983 - 1986):
Supervised staff of 15 administrative employees in a check printing facility. Directed all daily operations in such areas as personnel management, accounting, safety, audit preparation, billing, customer service, purchasing, security, attitude surveys, customer relations and P&L statements. Served as Sales/Plant Coordinator for 13 Sales Representatives in Colorado, Wyoming, Utah and Montana.
> *Accomplishments*: Heavily involved in planning and implementation of move into new printing facility. Received three "A's" on periodic plant audits. Developed new Employee Training Manual later utilized in three plants. Established procedure that reduced weekly billing errors by over 40%.

PLANT SUPERINTENDENT, Orlando, FL (1981 - 1983):
Directed activities of 50 production employees and five supervisors in a check printing facility. Managed production planning, scheduling, maintenance, quality control, inventory control and cost containment.
> *Accomplishments*: Increased operational efficiency by 12% per year. Improved delivery time from 79% to 93%. Established quality standards for employees, reducing rerun rate from 3.4% to 2.6%.

Education

MASTER OF BUSINESS ADMINISTRATION, concentration in accounting, University of Florida, 1989. GPA 3.8/4.0.

BACHELOR OF SCIENCE in Industrial Management, North Carolina State University, 1980. GPA 3.7/4.0.

References available on request.

SUSAN W. LINDSEY
5849 Bacchus Way
Richmond, Virginia 23226
(804) 355-0912

A results-oriented manager, with more than seven years of achievement in training, development and administration. Proficient in German and French. Available for travel and relocation.

OBJECTIVE
A management position in training and development or product support.

EDUCATION
BOSTON COLLEGE, Chestnut Hill, Massachusetts, 1980
BACHELOR OF ARTS in Education, *magna cum laude*
Dean's List, all semesters
Most Valuable Player, Water Polo, Fall 1976. Varsity Letter in Swimming.

PROFESSIONAL ABILITIES

TRAINING:
- Received special recognition for superior technical training of co-workers in specialized instructional strategies.
- Trained and supervised more than 150 workers in basic skills competence, providing effective corrective and positive feedback.
- Documented detailed policies and procedures to enhance delivery of organizational objectives.
- Effectively analyzed causes of worker performance problems; recommended, implemented and monitored the alternatives.
- Conducted ongoing performance appraisals at regular intervals.
- Motivated and coached workers to improve productivity and to achieve successful performance.

PROGRAM DESIGN:
- Organized, developed, implemented courseware and systems for work management, basics instruction and training development.
- Analyzed job tasks, established measurable objectives, tracked performance and successful completion of assignments.
- Created successful performance feedback systems and established system to monitor and record results.
- Planned and produced audio-visual courseware.
- Organized, planned and conducted educational tours, related to increasing job knowledge and performance.

COMMUNICATION SKILLS:
- Developed and delivered presentations to groups of up to 100 people.
- Counseled, interviewed and negotiated with co-workers, management, public officials and the general public to enhance inter-communication and working relationships.
- Edited reports, researched, composed and distributed written information and materials.

EMPLOYMENT HISTORY

1985 - 1990	Educator, Stuttgart, West Germany
	Department of Defense Dependent Schools
1980 - 1985	Educator, Richmond City Public School System

BARBARA B. ROSE

1899 Flagstone Road
Providence, RI 02906
(401) 874-7892

CAREER OBJECTIVE

A corporate position utilizing proven skills in organization and management.

SUMMARY OF QUALIFICATIONS

Strengths: More than ten years experience in planning, financing and administering business activities and fund raising events for several non-profit organiza - tions. Have well-developed skills in
* organizing and streamlining projects,
* managing personnel and delegating responsibility, and
* working within budgets and resources.

Education: University of Florida, Gainesville, FL
Bachelor of Arts in English, 1973
Graduated *cum laude*, GPA 3.63/4.0
Active in student government, sorority (Rush Chairperson and Treasurer) and volunteer civic projects.

EXPERIENCE HISTORY

ATLANTA HUMANE SOCIETY AUXILIARY
Elected as Board Member (1979 - 1989), Assistant Treasurer (1980) and Director (1986 - 1988). Organized and chaired three highly successful fund raisers.
* Originated and implemented new fund raiser ("County Fair") which has become an annual event.
* Was first chairperson to successfully operate Gift Shop at a profit.
* Operated "Casino Party" fund raiser within budget restrictions and exceeded all previous years in gross profits.

ATLANTA CHILDREN'S THEATRE GUILD
Served as Board Member (1978 - 1981), Events chairperson (1978) and Vice-President and Fund Raising Chairperson (1985).
* Investigated and negotiated sites for meetings and luncheons, and was responsible for artwork, printing and mailing invitations.
* Supervised five committees and thirty persons, who were responsible for catering, administration, decorations, transportation and gift shop for Christmas House Fund Raiser. Achieved highest profit to date.
* Established policies and procedures for gift shop, resulting in 50% increase in profit.

FIRST PRESBYTERIAN CHURCH
As Chairman of Christmas Pageant (1990), recruited volunteers, organized and directed par - ticipants, and initiated inclusion of other church classes.

REFERENCES AVAILABLE ON REQUEST.

WILLIAM L. EARLY
4002 Camellia Court
Rolling Meadows, Illinois 60008
(312) 395-3790

Objective   Senior manufacturing/engineering management position

Summary   Seven years senior management experience in manufacturing extending from factory operations to multi-facility responsibilities. Achievement in factory modernizations, tightly timed new product introductions and significant capacity increases. Expertise in cost reduction, quality improvement, materials, control, employee relations and strategic planning. Results oriented. MBA from the University of Chicago.

Experience   SCHWINN BICYCLE COMPANY, Chicago, Illinois, since 1986

Director of Manufacturing
Responsible for all domestic manufacturing for this leading bicycle manufacturer with plants in Wisconsin and Mississippi. Management responsibilities include materials requirements planning (MRP), capacity planning, staffing and industrial relations, quality assurance (QA), facility maintenance, automation planning, and cost management. Manage a staff of 200 through four direct reports and a budget of approximately $19 million. Report to the Chief Financial Officer.

Results:
• Assessed existing staff, reorganized where necessary and upgraded the professional factory staff.

• Upgraded the manufacturing process, virtually eliminating frame alignment defects, saving $228,000 annually.

• Doubled on-time delivery performance while increasing production volume by 45%.

• Developed a program to use temporary labor to offset cyclical market demands, saving the company $150,000 in labor costs.

• Managed the successful implementation of the manufacturing process for an all new state-of-the-art aluminum bike, the first entirely new (non-steel) bike in Schwinn's history.

• Installed cost control system enabling the organization to better measure factory expenses.

WILSON SPORTING GOODS COMPANY, River Grove, Illinois, 1980 - 1986

Director of Engineering Services

Managed a staff of 28 through four direct reports. Responsible for process automation, facilities engineering, industrial engineering, and operations planning in 13 domestic and foreign factories and four distribution centers. Reported to Senior Vice President, Operations.

Results:
* Established a manufacturing cost reduction program which saved more than $21 million during a five-year period (approximately 3% of the annual manufacturing costs).

* Accomplished a critical $3.7 million tennis ball capacity expansion in concert with the introduction of a blow molded tennis ball "can" and a new specialty product.

* Built a composite tennis racket factory in Kingstown, St. Vincent, and transferred the manufacturing equipment from the US in time to meet demanding production requirements.

* Responsible for $1.7 million of new process equipment and facilities which produced two new golf ball products against a tightly timed introductory schedule.

PROCTER & GAMBLE COMPANY, Cincinnati, Ohio and Jackson, Tennessee, 1971 - 1980

Engineering Manager, Jackson facility, 1978 - 1980

Results:
* Provided design services for automated cookie mix production.

* Accomplished energy conservation projects which reduced utility costs by 11%.

Operations Manager, Jackson facility, 1975 - 1977
Packaging Department Manager, Cincinnati, 1973 - 1975
Deodorizer Department Manager, Cincinnati, 1971 - 1973

Education   MBA, Executive Program, University of Chicago, 1985
BSIE, Georgia Institute of Technology, 1970

Honors: Tau Beta Pi - Engineering Honor Society
Alpha Pi Mu - Industrial Engineering Honor Society

WILLIAM D. BAXTER

231 South Street
Greenwood, SC 29661
(803) 684-2716

EXPERIENCE

ELMHURST CHEMICALS, Spartanburg, SC

Process Engineer (January 1986 - present):
Responsible for directing and controlling a number of distinct chemical processes, including blends and specialty chemicals for the plastics, automotive, and textile industries.

Achievements:
- Implemented a quality program that allows the middle 30% of a product's specifications to be obtained consistently.
- Implemented a statistical process control program on 25 products that has improved quality 15%.
- Aided in research and development of five new fiber finish products.
- Assisted in the design and start-up of a $400,000 capacity expansion for a polyolefin clarifier.
- Implemented a cost reduction program which cut total variable conversion costs by 9.6% for an annual savings of $75,000, with zero capital investment.
- Have completed 400 hours of continuing education in such areas as public speaking; computer training in Autocad, Lotus, and Wordperfect; statistics; Managerial Grid; Organic Chemistry; and CPR.

DEPENDABLE ENVIRONMENTAL SERVICES, INC., Atlanta, GA

Field Analytical Technician (Summers of 1984 and 1985):
Responsible for observation, documentation, and all sampling techniques on asbestos abatement projects, including project leader on major asbestos abatement projects in Memphis, TN and Charleston, SC.

EDUCATION

Bachelor of Science, Chemical Engineering, December, 1985
Georgia Institute of Technology, Atlanta, GA
Earned 75% of education expenses.

Honor Graduate, Secondary School, June 1981
St. Boniface Academy, Scarsdale, NY

Activities and honors:
- American Institute of Chemical Engineers, 1983 - 85
- Elected Board Member of Student Center, 1982 - 85
- Alpha Sigma Delta Phi Honor Society, 1981 - 82

REFERENCES AVAILABLE ON REQUEST.

MARK W. TANNER
5547 Roswell Road NE, Apt S-5
Atlanta, GA 30342
(404) 843-5678

Objective

To apply experience gained in management, physical therapy, and training to a corporate environment. Open for travel and relocation.

Experience

MANAGEMENT: More than seven years supervisory experience of up to ten employees. Interview and hire office and support staff. Handle accounting and bookkeeping functions, client liaison and sales/marketing strategies.

TRAINING: Train all clerical and administrative employees. Write and develop training programs for individual and client needs. Conduct lectures, seminars and platform training classes for up to fifty persons, including managers and other trainers. Highly skilled in one-on-one patient care and education.

GENERAL: Past employment has all involved extensive public contact and has required exceptional communicative skills, oral and written, on a variety of levels. Have developed excellent research skills.

Employment

Operations Manager, Goodhealth Fitness Center, Inc. (1987 - present): Hire, train, and supervise office and professional staff for Physical Therapy facility, which combines the benefits of medical expertise with an exercise center. Responsible for clinical aspects of patient care, education, class development, and progress evaluation. Also handle communications with physicians and other consulting professionals.

Prior employment has been as *Physical Therapist* for two major health centers, Dekalb General Hospital and Sinecure Health Center, conducting both in-patient and out-patient treatment.

Education

BACHELOR OF SCIENCE in Biology, University of South Carolina, 1980
Graduated *Phi Beta Kappa*

Certificate in Physical Therapy, University of Oklahoma, 1979.

Additional graduate-level courses taken at Georgia State University and Southern Technical Institute in Physical Therapy and Technical Writing.

Shaun H. McDonough
3580 Northside Drive NW
Atlanta, GA 30305
(404) 231-0988

Objective

Seeking career in Insurance and Risk Management. Long range career plans include training in several facets of the insurance industry, including Underwriting, Claims Adjusting, Loss Prevention, Risk Management, and other related fields. Immediate employment objective is a trainee position with a major insurance company.

Education

BACHELOR OF BUSINESS ADMINISTRATION in Risk Management and Insurance, University of Georgia, graduation planned for December, 1992.

Will graduate in the top 10% of the Business School.

Honors/activities: Dean's List several times, GPA 3.4/4.0, elected to membership in Beta Gamma Sigma (business honor society), recipient of academic scholarship for excellence in insurance curriculum, member of Collegiate Insurance Society.

Experience

Several years of _**retail sales**_ in family-owned clothing store during high school and college. Employed full-time during first year of college and during summers. Also assisted with formal _**bookkeeping**_ functions, including general ledger entries, accounts payable and receivable, payroll, and financial statements.

Most recently have been employed part-time at local distribution warehouse, in a shipping and receiving position.

Personal

Born November 17, 1970 . . . . . Married, no children . . . . . 5'10", 165 lb., excellent health . . . . . Open for travel and relocation . . . . . Interests and hobbies include physical fitness, reading, and personal investments.

References available on request.

(Sample references page)

SUSAN B. SWIFT
3829 Helen Lane
Durham, NC   27702
(919) 282-4837

REFERENCES

PATRICK M. JONES (client)
Purchasing Manager
North Carolina Food and Drug Distributors, Inc.
2173 Coventry Lane
Charlotte, NC   28760
(704) 822-9273

HAROLD T. HILL (former employer)
Southeast Region Sales Manager
Sunshine Foods, Inc.
7893 Chattahoochee Avenue SW
Atlanta, GA   30325
(404) 522-9754

BETTY W. REICHTER, CPA (personal)
Eastland, Wright and Morris, CPA's
8384 Holcombe Bridge Road
Chapel Hill, NC   28876
(919) 777-1829 - office
(919) 929-9293 - home

LLANA S. FRANCO

Temporary address:
348 Bulldog Drive
Athens, GA 30601
(404) 353-7621

Permanent Address:
1234 Azalea Road NW
Atlanta, GA 30327
(404) 262-7890

REFERENCES

Steve R. Smithe (summer internship supervisor)
Director of Marketing
IBM Corporation
1 Atlantic Center, Suite 3890
Atlanta, GA 30309
(404) 888-6255

Dr. Nancy M. Ethyl
Associate Professor of Business
University of Georgia
Athens, GA 30601
(404) 567-8238

Nancy T. Chapman (personal)
Director of Human Resources
ABC Corporation
872 Fourth Street
Atlanta, GA 30308
(404) 876-7725 - office
(404) 252-9872 - home

SAMPLE BUSINESS CARDS

GEOFFREY WILLIAMS
BBA, University of Georgia, 1991
Marketing major, 3.4 GPA
Dean's List, Intramural Sports, Fraternity President
Sales experience

3445 Piedmont Road NE, #R-3
Atlanta, GA 30342
(404) 278-7873

Human   Resources   Generalist

CHARLES T. RUTH
Recruiting • Benefits • Employee Relations
12 years experience

3890 Teagle Road, Mobile, AL   36588
(205)   981-3169

BS/MS, Mechanical Engineering
Seven years manufacturing experience

JAMES P. NELSON
Pepsico   (1989 - 1992)
Proctor & Gamble   (1985 - 1989)

248 Main Street, Milwaukee, WI   78906
(888)   111-1111

SUZANNE HOYETTE, C.P.A.
Accounting and Financial Management
10 years experience
Seeking position as Corporate Controller

231 E. Atlantic Street, South Hill, VA 23970
(804) 447-8746

Communications Specialist
Spanish Bilingual

JOY K. BAER
345 Cloverhill Lane
Decatur, GA 30303
(404) 377-0987

B.A. Journalism, 1981
M.A. Communications, 1985

MARY W. SMILEY
B.B.A., Management, 1987
First Lieutenant, US Army, 1987 - 1991
Materials Management

8943 Roswell Road NE, Roswell, GA 30076
(404) 789-3333

APPENDIX B: CORRESPONDENCE

All job-related correspondence should conform to these two rules:

(1) Keep it brief, relevant, and to the point.

(2) Make it as personal as possible.

The following cover letters and thank-you notes illustrate those principles. In addition, observe that they are very positive in tone, with an emphasis on achievements and accomplishments.

Finally, remember your purpose in writing these correspondences:

• Including a cover letter with your resume is to create a good, strong first impression and thus get your resume read.

• If you include a separate salary history page, your purpose is not only to relay information requested, but also to continue on the positive track created through your cover letter and resume.

• A thank-you note should express your interest in the position and reinforce the positive impression you made during your interview.

Keeping those objectives in mind will help you compose your documents.

(Cover Letter Sample 1)

1234 Pineland Drive NW
Atlanta, GA 30327
September 28, 1989

Procter & Gamble Distributing Company
7890 Tide Road
Butler, GA 30345

Dear Sirs:

In response to your recent advertisement for a distribution management
position, I am enclosing my resume. As you will see from my
experiences, I am an over-achiever with a demonstrated pattern of success.

In addition to my B.B.A. in Operations Management, which I entirely
self-financed, I have five years of distribution-related experience in the
areas that you specified in your ad. As a First Lieutenant in the US Army,
I supervised more than forty persons in the operation of a large
distribution center, including shipping/receiving, warehousing, inventory
control and material management. I received outstanding evaluations and
Officer Efficiency Reports.

Thank you for your time and consideration, and I look forward to
hearing from you soon. I am available for interviews immediately.

Sincerely yours,

Albert E. Joshua
(404) 255-3456

(Cover Letter Sample 2)

TIM G. HALL
876 Sprayberry Lane
Charlotte, NC 28241

November 17, 1991

Ms. Robin Henry
Human Resources Manager
Union Camp Corporation
4341 Paper Bag Lane
Savannah, GA 31404

Dear Ms. Henry:

I am enclosing my resume and salary history in response to your recent advertisement for a Marketing Development Manager. I am additionally familiar with Union Camp through Bill Smith, one of your Sales Managers in Savannah, and a former business associate. We worked together on a quality control problem at our company's Miami facility, and he has offered to be one of my references.

I have eight years of highly successful sales and promotion experience in the wood products industry. I have exceeded my weekly sales quotas by 40%, resulting in a total sales increase of 18%. I attribute this success to my strong problem-solving and interpersonal skills, and my ability to develop a close and creditable relationship with my customers.

Thank you for your time and consideration, and I will call you in a few days to confirm that you have received my resume. As your advertisement requested, I have enclosed my salary history. I am available for an interview at your convenience.

Sincerely yours,

Tim Hall
(704) 237-8724

(Cover Letter Sample 3)

ANNA K. DEHOFF

1594 Arden Rd NW
Atlanta, GA 30327
(404) 264-8631

February 23, 1991

Ms. Deborah Beagle
ABC Software Development Company
100 Peachtree St NE
Suite 2104
Asheville, NC 28255

Dear Ms. Beagle:

I am a college graduate in Computer Management and have two years programming experience. I am writing to you to inquire if you have present or projected needs in my field, and I have enclosed my resume for your perusal.

During my two years with XYZ Corporation, I have been rated a "5," which is the highest evaluation possible.

Thank you for your time and consideration. I would appreciate the opportunity to meet with you at your earliest convenience and look forward to hearing from you soon.

Sincerely,

Anna K. DeHoff

(Cover Letter Sample 4)

879 Ridge Point Drive
Smyrna, GA 30339
April 7, 1991

Mr. John Thompson, Director of Personnel
Chicken Little Company
456 Corn Street
College Park, GA 30365

Dear Mr. Thompson:

Thank you for your time on the phone today and for the information regarding your current need for an Industrial Engineer. As you requested, I am enclosing my resume for your review.

During my three years with ABC Textiles, I have been responsible for implementing and managing projects very similar to the ones you described to me. A few of my recent assignments include these:
    -- Organized and conducted a study to determine and document causes of dye department downtime.
    -- Designed, estimated cost and proposed layout for relocation of maintenance shop, resulting in a 20% increase in efficiency.
    -- Assisted Safety Department in training employees on the proper use of new machinery, resulting in a decrease of 25% in time lost due to accidents.

Thank you again, and I look forward to hearing from you soon. My current salary is $37,000 annually, and I am available for relocation.

Sincerely yours,

Lynn K. Parsons
(404) 433-4898

(Cover Letter Sample 5)

4011 Roswell Rd NE, #F-6
Atlanta, GA 30342
November 18, 1992

Cartwell Chemical Company
7890 Riviera Parkway
Jacksonville, FL 32306

Dear Sirs:

Under my direction, production planning has been optimized at multiple facilities, including contract manufacturers and overseas facilities.

As you are advertising for an experienced Department Manager, you may be interested in my qualifications:
-- As Inventory Control Manager, I reduced inventories from $50M to $42M, while improving product availability.
-- I designed and implemented a material recovery program that saved more than $175,000 annually.
-- Working with the MIS Department, I installed a new computerized database and operating program, substantially reducing inventory loss.

In addition, I have a Master's degree in management and a Bachelor's degree in chemistry.

Thank you for your time and consideration, and I will call you soon to confirm that you have received my resume. My enclosed salary history reflects consistent salary promotions in all positions held. I am available for interviews at your convenience.

Sincerely yours,

Celia Mosier
(404) 250-1234

(Cover Letter Sample 6)

4488 Rembrandt Lane
Charlottesville, VA   23932
January 22, 1992

Ms. Shiela DelRag, Region Sales Manager
Agnes Laboratories, Inc.
3333 Scott Parkway
Decatur, GA   30030

Dear Ms. DelRag:

I am contacting you at the suggestion of Mike Douglas, the ABC Laboratories Sales Representative who handles our account.   I am seeking to make a career change, out of purchasing and into a medical sales position. My resume is enclosed for your perusal.

My five years of experience as a hospital purchasing agent has given me valuable insight into the problems encountered by both your sales force and their clients, and I believe that knowledge will be most helpful in my new career.   In addition, I have recently received my Bachelor's degree in marketing, while employed full-time at Carolinas' Medical Center.

I realize that my current salary of $32,000 may be higher than the salary generally offered to entry-level sales representatives, and thus I am flexible in my compensation requirements. My primary concern now is to establish a career in medical sales.

I trust my experience and initiative will be desirable attributes for ABC Laboratories, and I will call you next week to answer any questions you may have. I am available for an interview at your convenience.

Sincerely yours,

John G. Taylor
(703) 896-3748

(Sample Broadcast Letter)

MICHAEL FOSTER
640 Habersham Road NW
Atlanta, GA 30305
(404) 233-8433

April 18, 1992

Mr. Jim Nelson
Flight Simulations, Inc.
246 Park View Ave.
Chicago, IL 60634

Dear Mr. Nelson,

As Manager of Marketing, I initiated a fundamental change in product development strategy which led to a 31% increase in market share.

I am writing you because I am certain I would have similar results working in your organization. A few of my other achievements follow:

- Developed and executed marketing plans which led to a 175% increase in international sales in two years.
- Positioned and launched three new product lines which account for more than 90% of sales volume.
- Lowered the cost per unit of advertising and sales support material by 50% while maintaining quality and effectiveness.
- Lowered the cost of market research by 80% through more efficient use of internal resources.
- Increased inventory turnover 15% through use of refined forecasting techniques.

I have an MBA and fifteen years of professional experience.

I would welcome the opportunity to discuss my background further. Please call at your earliest convenience.

Sincerely,

Michael Foster
(404) 233-8433

LAURIE T. ST. JOHN

3345 Lindberg Road NE
Atlanta, GA 30324
(404) 262-7331

SALARY HISTORY

Bruce D. Morgan & Associates, Importers (1981 - Present):

National Sales Manager (1986 - present)
$57,500 salary + commission + bonus

Region Sales Manager (1983 - 1986)
$35,000 salary + commission

Sales Representative (1981 - 1983)
$18,000 salary + commission

All positions included company car and expense account.

Seeking initial total compensation of $75,000. Long range advancement and income incentives are paramount. Will consider lower salary/draw with high commission potential.

Edmond R. Smith

1200 Franklin Road NE, Apt. F-1
Charlotte, NC 28754
(404) 847-1234

Salary History

Western Union Telegraph Company (December 1984 - present)

Senior Internal Auditor (4/89 - present)	$ 41,150
Supervisor Financial Control (4/87 - 4/89)	39,600
Regional Staff Manager (11/85 - 4/87)	37,150
Internal Audit Supervisor (12/84 - 11/85)	32,300

E. L. Lowie & Company (December 1981 - November 1984)

Assistant Controller	$26,500

Convenient Systems, Inc. (October 1979 - November 1981)

Divisional Controller (8/77 - 11/78)	$21,000
Accounting Manager (9/76 - 8/77)	15,600

A. M. Pullen & Company (June 1976 - September 1979) $13,500

LURLINE C. HARRIS

231 E. Atlantic Street
South Hill, VA 23970
(804) 447-8746

SALARY HISTORY

Synergism Systems (March 1987 - present)

Director of Compensation and Benefits $55,000

Citizens and Southern National Bank (May 1984 - March 1987)
Senior Compensation Analyst $47,000
Compensation Analyst   42,000
Exempt Recruiter   35,000

(Note: Income reduction accepted in order to enter
corporate Human Resources.)

Blinders Personnel Service (July 1981 - May 1984)

Accounting Division Manager $49,000
Senior Recruiter   40,000
Staff Recruiter   18,000

(Thank-you Note Sample 1)

231 E. Atlantic Street
South Hill, VA 23970
June 17, 1992

Mr. Thomas C. Browder
Hillside Energy and Automation
235 Peachtree St NE
Suite 2330
Atlanta, GA 30303

Dear Mr. Browder,

Thank you and your staff for the time you spent with me today. I very much enjoyed learning more about Hillside Energy and Automation and the new compensation program you are developing. With my five years of compensation and benefits experience, I am certain I can give excellent direction to your program and would greatly enjoy the challenge.

I am enclosing an article from the recent edition of <u>Compensation Today</u>, which describes a compensation program similar to the one we discussed. I thought it might be of interest to you.

Thank you again, and I look forward to hearing from you soon.

Sincerely yours,

Lurline C. Harris
(804) 447-8746

(Thank-you Note Sample 2)

LLANA S. FRANCO

Temporary address:
348 Bulldog Drive
Athens, GA 30601
(404) 353-7621

Permanent Address:
1234 Azalea Road NW
Atlanta, GA 30327
(404) 262-7890

April 21, 1990

Mr. Wynn Patterholm
Wachovia Bank of Georgia
191Peachtree St NE
Suite 1234
Atlanta, GA 30303

Dear Mr. Patterholm,

As a recent college graduate, I realize that although my business experience is indeed limited, my potential is vast! My achievements and accomplishments to date illustrate the pattern of success I am certain I will continue.

Thank you for your interview time today at the University of Georgia's Career Day. I am very interested in Wachovia's Management Development Program, and I feel that I have much to contribute. I look forward to hearing from you soon. After graduation on May 21, I can be contacted at the permanent address above.

Sincerely yours,

Wendy C. Bloom

(Thank-you Note Sample 3)

MARTIN J. SHELLYS

1976 October Street
Cartersville, GA 31655

April 12, 1990

Ms. Jan Cotton
Mobil Chemical Company
P O Box 78
Covington, GA 30302

Dear Ms. Cotton,

Thank you for your time and information yesterday, and especially for the tour of your facility. With your state-of-the-art equipment, I can easily understand why Mobil Chemical has been so successful, and I would like the opportunity to contribute to that success.

As I stated during our interview, I have been the top sales representative in my district with Scott Paper Company for the past three years. That achievement illustrates the abilities I also could bring to Mobil.

Thank you for your consideration. I am available for further interviews at your convenience.

Sincerely yours,

Martin J. Shellys
(404) 928-5673

APPENDIX C:

Detailed Profiles of Selected Companies

The following employers are among the largest hiring companies in the Triangle and Triad region. These companies were selected primarily based on the large number of salaried (versus hourly) and professional-level employees hired annually, but also for diversity and variety. In developing a direct contact marketing strategy, these are the ones you should contact on your own. Smaller companies that hire only a few employees each year are not a good source to direct contact, unless you have specific experience in their industry. The Career Search System includes other sources to reach those smaller companies.

I believe that we have included here every company in the Triad and Triangle that hires 20+ professional-level employees each year, but if you encounter one we omitted, please let me know. One exception to this, however, is that there are certain industries (*e.g.*, fast foods) and specialties (*e.g.*, health care) for which there are nearly infinite needs. I have not tried to include all of those hiring companies, but rather a few of the largest.

EXPLANATION OF TERMINOLOGY

This book is primarily for career-oriented, "white-collar" employees, most often with a college degree (although not always or necessarily), and thus the positions I am describing are of that level. I have frequently made use of the terms "**exempt**" and "**non-exempt**" in describing positions, and unless you have worked in a personnel

247

department, you may not be familiar with their meaning. These terms relate to the federal wage and salary laws, and to avoid boring you with a lengthy explanation of a complex system, just remember that generally speaking, most on-going career positions with executive potential are called "exempt" (that is, they are exempt from the federal wage and salary laws), although there are numerous exceptions. For example, banks frequently hire individuals into non-exempt Teller positions, and then promote into exempt positions when one occurs. Other companies like to hire recent college grads in non-exempt positions, in order to learn their business "from the bottom up."

This explanation may seem irrelevant to you now, but since it does affect your time and income, I have noted it in my company descriptions. Also knowing the number of exempt employees at a specific company will give you a general idea of the career potential there.

Another term you may not understand is "**MIS**," the abbreviation for Management Information Systems, and which has become a generally accepted acronym for data processing and computer positions.

DISCLAIMER

The information contained herein was obtained from company officials and/or published sources, and is believed to be accurate. However, the author and publisher assume no liability for errors or the consequences thereof. Employment figures are generally approximate and can fluctuate. I would greatly appreciate information regarding any errors or omissions, and comments about any companies contained here. Send any information to P O Box 52291, Atlanta, GA 30355.

SELECTED COMPANIES

Note: See proceeding page for explanation of terms used

AETNA LIFE & CASUALTY
Profile: One of the nation's largest insurance companies employing nearly 800 here with 25% exempt. Recent grads primarily hired for the claims department. Normally promotes from within but occasionally has needs for experienced personnel.
Procedure: Send resume to Human Resources,
#3 Centerview Dr., Greensboro, NC 27407
(910) 854-2050

ALLSTATE INSURANCE
Profile: Support and sales staff for this national property and casualty insurance company. Employs around 150 in this office. Hires recent grads for claims positions. Looks for experienced personnel for sales jobs.
Procedure: Send resume to Human Resources,
3100 Spring Forest Rd., Suite 800 (Esther), Raleigh, NC 27609
(919) 560-2000

AMERICAN EXPRESS - TRAVEL RELATED SERVICES
Profile: Telephone support center for this financial services firm. Employs 2,500 here with nearly 300 exempt. Hires recent grads into customer service positions. Has few needs for experienced exempt personnel since they like to promote from within.
Procedure: Send resume to Human Resources,
6500 Airport Parkway, Greensboro, NC 27409
(910) 668-5195

AMP INCORPORATED
Profile: National manufacturer and distributor of electronic devices. Employs nearly 1,000 in the Triad area. Seeks both recent

grads and experienced personnel in engineering (electrical, mechanical).

Procedure: Send resume to Human Resources,
3700 Reidsville Rd., Winston-Salem, NC 27102
(910) 725-9222

ARK-LES CORPORATION

Profile: Manufacturer of switching devices employing about 270 in the Triangle. Primarily seeks manufacturing engineers -- both recent grads and experienced professionals.

Procedure: Send resume to Human Resources,
3400 Yonkers Rd., Raleigh, NC 27620
(919) 231-2000

ARTHUR ANDERSEN & CO.

Profile: "Big Six" CPA firm with large consulting operation. Employs about 80 in this office. Hires about 10 recent grads into its audit/tax division and 10 recent grads into the consulting division yearly. Rarely seeks experienced personnel.

Procedure: Send resume to Recruiter,
One Hanover Sq., Suite 1100, Raleigh, NC 27601
(919) 832-5400

ATLANTIC NETWORKING SYSTEMS

Profile: A local and wide area networking firm employing close to 30 people. Has needs for sales people with 2-5 years of experience and a degree in electrical engineering. Not interested in recent grads.

Procedure: Send resume to Human Resources,
975 Walnut St., Suite 104, Cary, NC 27511
(919) 469-8155

AT&T FEDERAL SYSTEMS

Profile: Primarily provides underwater surveillance equipment for the Navy. Employs nearly 3,000 here but are currently undergoing a downsizing. Seeks experienced personnel in engineering (EM, ME), accounting, and MIS.

Procedure: Send resume to Human Resources,
PO Box 20046, Greensboro, NC 27420

(910) 279-7000

AT&T NETWORK SYSTEMS
Profile: Provider of business translation services as well as customer education and training. Employs 375 with approximately 300 exempt level. Hires both recent grads and experienced personnel in all languages for its translation services.

Procedure: Send resume to Human Resources,
2400 Reynolda Rd., Winston-Salem, NC 27106
(910) 727-3100

BASF CORPORATE AGRICULTURAL PRODUCTS
Profile: Develops and manufactures plant protection products. Employs 225 with roughly 50% exempt level. Has needs for recent chemistry grads - especially those with an associate degree. Rarely seeks experienced personnel.

Procedure: Send resume to Human Resources,
2505 Meridian Parkway, Durham, NC 27713
(919) 248-6500

BB&T (GREENSBORO)
Profile: Regional commercial and retail bank headquartered in Wilson, NC. Employs about 500 in Greensboro with roughly 33% exempt. Hires recent grads and MBAs for its management training program. Promotes from within and rarely seeks experienced personnel.
Note: BB&T recently merged with Southern National.

Procedure: Send resume to Human Resources,
PO Box 26122, Greensboro, NC 27402
(910) 574-5602

BB&T (RALEIGH)
Profile: Regional commercial and retail bank headquartered in Wilson, NC. Employs about 175 here with 30% exempt level. Hires recent grads and MBAs for its management training program. Rarely seeks experienced personnel.

Procedure: Send resume to Human Resources,
434 Fayetteville St. Mall, Raleigh, NC 27611
(919) 831 4000

BTI

Profile: Growing long distance telephone company employing close to 180 in the Triangle and Triad. Hires a couple of recent grads per year into customer support positions. Seeks experienced telecommunications personnel in all areas.

Procedure: Send resume to Human Resources,
PO Box 150002, Raleigh, NC 27624
(919) 872-9100

BECTON DICKINSON & CO.

Profile: Health care products research firm employing roughly 160. Rarely hires recent grads. Seeks personnel with 3-5 years experience in biochemistry, biotechnology, and materials sciences.

Procedure: Send resume to Human Resources,
21 Davis Dr., RTP, NC 27709
(919) 549-8641

BLUE CROSS BLUE SHIELD OF NORTH CAROLINA

Profile: National health insurance provider. This office employs about 2,000 with about 33% exempt level. Seeks both recent grads and experienced for programmer analysts, sales reps, insurance specialties (claims, actuarial), and accounting/finance.

Procedure: Send resume to Personnel,
PO Box 2291, Durham, NC 27702-2291
(919) 490-2850

BELL NORTHERN RESEARCH (BNR)

Profile: Northern Telecom subsidiary conducting research and development for telecommunications equipment and systems. Employs 1,200 here, with about 50% exempt level. Seeks recent grads and experienced personnel in computer science and computer engineering.

Procedure: Send resume to Human Resources,
35 Davis Dr., RTP, NC 27709
(919) 991-7000

BOWMAN GRAY MEDICAL SCHOOL

Profile:
Medical school affiliated with Wake Forest University and Baptist Hospital. Employs 3,000+ with nearly 50% exempt. Hires recent grads for accounting/finance, computer science, biochemistry. Hires MBAs as project management assistants. Hires experienced personnel for human resources, lab technicians, and management.

Procedure:
Send resume to Human Resources, Medical Center Blvd., Winston-Salem, NC 27517-1017 (910) 716-4255; job hotline: 716-3742

BRISTOL MYERS PRODUCTS

Profile:
National pharmaceutical manufacturer. Employs 600 here. Rarely hires recent grads. Hires experienced personnel for manufacturing engineering, operations management, and chemistry.

Procedure:
Send resume to Human Resources, 9707 Chapel Hill Rd., Morrisville, NC 27560 (919) 319-7800

BROADBAND TECHNOLOGIES

Profile:
Provider of telecommunications equipment employing about 250 in the Triangle with about 75% exempt. Hires very few recent grads - looks for 2-year tech degrees. Hires a few experienced personnel for computer engineering and software and hardware development.

Procedure:
Send resume to Human Resources, PO Box 13737, RTP, NC 27709 (919) 544-0015

BURROUGHS WELLCOME - R&D

Profile:
Provides research and development for this major pharmaceutical manufacturer. Employs 1,000+, mostly exempt. Hires PhD's in organic chemistry, chemistry, psychobiology, and behavioral psychology.

Procedure:
Send resume to Human Resources, 3030 Cornwallis Rd., RTP, NC 27709 (919) 248-3000; job hotline: (919) 248-8347

BURROUGHS WELLCOME - SALES & MARKETING
Profile: Markets and distributes pharmaceuticals. Employs 1,000 with most reps out in the field. Rarely hires recent grads. Has sales development program for MBAs. Has needs for experienced sales people.

Procedure: Send resume to Human Resources,
3030 Cornwallis Rd., RTP, NC 27709
(919) 248-3000; job hotline: (919) 248-8347

CAROLINA MEDICORP, INC.
Profile: Runs Forsyth Memorial Hospital, the largest hospital in Winston-Salem employing 4,500+. Seeks both recent grads and experienced personnel in all medical specialties - especially clinical areas. Experienced exempt needs are in accounitng/finance.

Procedure: Send resume to Human Resources,
3333 Silas Creek Pkwy., Winston-Salem, NC 27104
(910) 718-2800

CAROLINA POWER & LIGHT
Profile: Regional electronic utility company employing nearly 2,000 in the Triangle. Hires 20+ recent grads each year, usually for nuclear engineering. Seeks experienced personnel in human resources, MIS, accounting/finance.

Procedure: Send resume to Human Resources,
411 Fayetteville St., Raleigh, NC 27602
(919) 546-6111

CENTRAL CAROLINA BANK
Profile: Regional commercial and retail bank employing 1,200 in the Triangle with about 25% exempt. Hires about 10 recent grads each year for its management training program. Has few needs for experienced personnel -- will usually promote from within.

Procedure: Send resume to Human Resources,
111 Corcoran St., Durham, NC 27702
(919) 683-7777

CENTURA

Profile: Regional retail and commercial bank with 30 branches in the
              Triangle. Hires between 5-7 recent grads per year for its
              management training program. Has occasional needs for
              experienced banking professionals.
Procedure: Send resume to Human Resources,
              PO Box 1220, Rocky Mount, NC 27802
              (919) 977-4037

CIBA-GEIGY CORPORATION - CHEMICALS DIVISION

Profile: Develops and markets performance chemicals and additives.
              Employs about 65 in this division. Has needs for Ph.D.'s in
              chemistry for its paper and pulp products. Seeks experienced
              personnel in accounting/finance, sales, and human resources.
Procedure: Send resume to Human Resources (Chemicals Division)
              PO Box 18300, Greensboro, NC 27409
              (910) 632-2629

CIBA-GEIGY - CORPORATE DIVISION

Profile: Provides other divisions of Ciba with technical support.
              Employs about 200 in this division. Occasionally hires recent
              grads as lab technicians and for MIS (IBM). Has few needs
              for experienced personnel.
Procedure: Send resume to Human Resources (Corporate Division),
              PO Box 183000, Greensboro, NC 27409
              (910) 632-6000

CIBA-GEIGY - TEXTILE PRODUCTS

Profile: Produces textile products. Employs 425 in this division. Hires
              a couple of recent chemistry grads per year and also runs an
              internship program. Has needs for experienced personnel in
              accounting/finance and human resources.
Procedure: Send resume to Human Resources (Textile Products),
              PO Box 18300, Greensboro, NC 27409
              (910) 632-6000

COASTAL HEALTHCARE

Profile: National provider of physician contract management services
              to hospitals and healthcare institutions. Employs roughly

3,000. Hires MBAs into healthcare management. Has needs for experienced personnel in accounting/finance, MIS, management.

Procedure: Send resume to Human Resources,
2828 Croasdaile Dr., Durham, NC 27704
(919) 383-0355

COCA-COLA BOTTLING OF GREENSBORO

Profile: Triad soft drink distributor employing close to 100 here. Hires recent grads into sales and management training. Has occasional needs for experienced personnel in accounting/finance, sales, and management.

Procedure: Send resume to Human Resources,
8200 Capital Dr., Greensboro, NC 27409
(910) 665-1919

COCA-COLA BOTTLING COMPANY, CONSOLIDATED

Profile: Triangle soft drink distributor employing about 120 in the area. Hires recent grads as route sales trainees. Most other recruiting done out of Charlotte.

Procedure: Send resume to Human Resources,
2200 S. Wilmington St., Raleigh, NC 27603
(919) 834-2551
For Charlotte: Send resume to Human Resources,
PO Box 31487, Charlotte, NC 28231; (704) 551-4400

COLLEGE FOUNDATION

Profile: Non-profit service institution providing student loans. Employs 150+, with about 25% exempt. Hires recent grads for accounting/finance, sales, MIS. Rarely has openings for experienced personnel.

Procedure: Send resume to Human Resources,
2100 Yonkers Rd., Raleigh, NC 27605
(919) 834-2893

COMPUCHEM LABORATORIES

Profile: Provides environmental and forensic drug testing. Employs about 400 with close to 50% exempt level. Hires recent grads in chemistry, biology, zoology. Usually promotes from within and has few needs for experienced personnel.

Procedure: Send resume to Human Resources,
3308 Chapel Hill-Nelson Highway, RTP, NC 27709
(919) 549-8263

COMPUTER INTELLIGENCE, INC.

Profile: Provides computer software services and employs about 135. Hires both recent grads and experienced personnel mostly for computer science.

Procedure: Send resume to Human Resources,
PO Box 98990, Raleigh, NC 27624
(919) 676-8300

CONE MILLS COPRORATION

Profile: Major national textile manufacturer employing 3,000+ in the Triad area. Hires recent grads for accounting/finance, sales, management, engineering, MIS. Rarely seeks experienced personnel.

Procedure: Send resume to Human Resources,
1201 Maple St., Greensboro, NC 27405
(910) 379-6220

COOPERS & LYBRAND

Profile: One of the "Big Six" Accounting and consulting firms. Employs close to 100 here, mostly exempt. Hires about 10 recent CPA graduates each year. Rarely seeks experienced personnel as it usually promotes from within and transfers in and out of other offices.

Procedure: Send resume to Recruiter,
150 Fayetteville St. Mall, Suite 2300, Raleigh, NC 27601
(919)755-3000

DELOITTE & TOUCHE

Profile: One of the "Big Six" international CPA firms employing 85 in this office. Hires about 10-12 recent CPA grads each year. Usually hires experienced personnel from other D&T offices.

Procedure: Send resume to Recruiting Director,

First Union Capital Center, Suite 1800, 10 Fayetteville St.
Mall, Raleigh, NC 27601
(919) 546-8000

DOROTHEA DIX HOSPITAL

Profile: State run psychiatric hospital employing 1,500 with about 25% exempt. Rarely hires recent grads. Seeks experienced psychiatrists, RNs, and social workers. Non-exempt entry level positions done through Employment Security Commission.

Procedure: Send resume to Personnel,
820 S. Boylan Ave., Raleigh, NC 27603
(919) 733-5540

DUKE UNIVERSITY

Profile: Private university in Durham employing nearly 8,000. Seeks both recent grads and experienced personnel for accounting/finance, MIS, management.

Procedure: Send resume to Human Resources,
Erwin Rd., Durham, NC 27710
(919) 684-2015

DUKE UNIVERSITY MEDICAL CENTER

Profile: Largest medical facility in North Carolina employing nearly 13,000. Hires 300+ exempt annually. Seeks both recent grads and experienced personnel in accounting/finance, hospital management, MIS (IBM), and all medical specialties.

Procedure: Send resume to Human Resources,
Erwin Rd., Durham, NC 27710
(919) 684-2015

DUN & BRADSTREET CORPORATION

Profile: Nation's largest information gathering service company employing close to 100 in this office. Seeks recent grads as business analysts and sales people. Rarely seeks experienced personnel.

Procedure: Send resume to Human Resources,
2000 Pisgah Church Rd., Greensboro, NC 27455
(910) 282-4500

DURHAM COUNTY HOSPITAL
Profile: Veterans Affairs hospital employing about 2,200 with about 25% exempt. Hires a few recent grads in medicine, accounting/finance, and MIS. Seeks experienced personnel in accounting/finance, computer science, and MIS.

Procedure: Send resume to Human Resources,
3643 N. Roxboro Rd., Durham, NC 27704
(919) 470-4000

DURHAM HERALD CO., INC.
Profile: Publisher of the daily Durham Herald Sun, employing 380 with about 45% exempt. Seeks both recent grads and experienced personnel for management and sales. Looks for experience in its editorial staff.

Procedure: Send resume to Human Resources,
PO Box 2092, Durham, NC 27702
(919) 419-6500

DURHAM PUBLIC SCHOOLS
Profile: Primary school district in Durham employing close to 4,000 with 1,800 teachers. Seldom hires recent grads. Hires 20+ experienced personnel in accounting/finance for its support services. Has experience requirements for teachers.

Procedure: Send resume to Human Resources,
PO Box 30002, Durham, NC 27702
(919) 560-2000

ELECTRONIC DATA SYSTEMS (EDS)
Profile: Data processing and computing subsidiary of General Motors employing 310 in Raleigh. Seeks both recent grads and experienced personnel for program analysts, accounting/finance, and MIS.

Procedure: Send resume to EDS Staffing,
200 Galleria Park, Suite 910, Atlanta, GA 30339
Raleigh: 4800 Six Forks Rd., Raleigh, NC 27619
(919) 783-8000

EDWARD VALVES, INC.

Profile:	Designer and producer of valves employing about 200 in Raleigh. Seeks both recent grads and experienced personnel for engineering (design, mechanical). Occasionally seeks experienced personnel for accounting/finance.
Procedure:	Send resume to Human Resources, 1900 S. Saunders St., Raleigh, NC 27602 (919) 832-0525

ERNST & YOUNG

Profile:	"Big Six" CPA firm employing about 130 here, mostly exempt. Hires about 15 MBAs per year for its consulting business. Occasionally has needs for experienced personnel, but usually fills needs from other E&Y offices.
Procedure:	Send resume to Recruiting Director, 3200 Beachleaf Court., Suite 700, Raleigh, NC 27604 (919) 981-2800

FGI

Profile:	Integrated marketing company (advertising, public relations) employing about 120, mostly exempt. Has occasional needs for recent grads in entry level advertising positions (account assistant, traffic, production assistant). Seeks experienced personnel in various advertising and PR positions.
Procedure:	Send resume to Human Resources, 206 W. Franklin St., Chapel Hill, NC 27516 (919) 932-8800

FIRST CITIZEN'S BANK (Raleigh)

Profile:	State wide bank and mortgage company employing 1,200+ with about 25% exempt. Hires recent grads and MBAs for its management training programs in commercial and retail banking. Rarely has needs for experienced personnel.
Procedure:	Send resume to Human Resources, 239 Fayetteville St. Mall, Raleigh, NC 27611 (919) 755-7000

FIRST CITIZEN'S BANK (Greensboro)

Profile:	State wide bank and mortgage company employing close to 100 in Greensboro with 25% exempt. Hires recent grads and

MBAs for its management training programs in commercial and retail banking. Rarely has needs for experienced personnel.

Procedure: Send resume to Human Resources,
239 Fayetteville St. Mall, Raleigh, NC 27611
(919) 755-7000
Greensboro: 100 S. Elm St., Greensboro, NC 27402
(910) 271-4000

FIRST UNION NATIONAL BANK OF NORTH CAROLINA

Profile: Super-regional bank headquartered in Charlotte employing about 150 in Greensboro with 30% exempt. Hires recent grads for customer service and teller positions locally. Management trainee programs handled through Charlotte. Rarely has needs for experienced personnel.

Procedure: Send resume to Human Resources,
PO Box 21965, Greensboro, NC 27420; (910) 378-4011
Charlotte: 1400 One First Union Center, Charlotte, NC 28288; (704) 374-6565

FIRST UNION MORTGAGE CORPORATION

Profile: Subsidiary of First Union providing mortgage services employing 800 here in Raleigh. Hires recent grads for customer service, research, and collections. Seeks experienced personnel with mortgage banking background.

Procedure: Send resume to Human Resume,
150 Fayetteville St. Mall, Raleigh, NC 27601
(919) 881-6000

FIRST WACHOVIA CORPORATION

Profile: Third largest bank in North Carolina, one of the three super-regionals headquartered in North Carolina. Employs 3,000+ with about 30% exempt level. Hires 60-70 recent grads per year into all areas of banking (retail, corporate, operations, information services). Also hires 15+ MBAs into management programs. Has occasional needs for experienced personnel in all areas of banking.

Procedure: Send resume to Human Resources,
301 N. Main St., Winston Salem, NC 27150

(910) 770-5000

FORSYTH TECHNICAL COMMUNITY COLLEGE
Profile: Local technical college employing 500+ with about 25% exempt. Hires recent grads in accounting/finance and MIS. Seeks experienced personnel in accounting/finance. Seeks teachers in all technical disciplines.

Procedure: Send resume to Human Resources,
2100 Silas Creek Pkwy., Winston-Salem, NC 27103
(910) 723-0371

GE CAPITAL MORTGAGE CORPORATION
Profile: Provider of mortgage insurance employing 500+ here in Raleigh. Hires a few recent grads each year for its management training program. Seeks experienced personnel in accounting/finance, management, and MIS.

Procedure: Send resume to Human Resources,
6601 Six Forks Rd., Raleigh, NC 27619

(919) 846-4100

GILBARCO, INC.
Profile: Designs and produces service station equipment. Employs about 1,500 here with about 40% exempt level. Hires both recent grads and experienced personnel for engineering (ME, EE, IE). Seeks additional experienced personnel for sales.

Procedure: Send resume to Human Resources,
7300 W. Friendly Ave., Greensboro, NC 27420
(910) 547-5000

GLAXO INC.
Profile: Research facility for this UK based pharmaceutical giant. Employs about 3,500 here. Seeks both recent grads and experienced personnel for accounting/finance and pharmaceutical research positions. Also maintains a co-op program involving its research division.

Procedure: Send resume to Human Resources,
5 Moore Dr., RTP, NC 27709
(919) 248-2100

GLOBAL SOFTWARE, INC.

Profile: Contractor of computer software support employing about 250, mostly exempt. Hires both recent grads and experienced personnel for computer science and accounting/finance.

Procedure: Send resume to Human Resources,
1009 Spring Forest Rd., Raleigh, NC 27615
(919) 872-7800

GODWIN, BOOKE, & DICKINSON

Profile: Employee benefit consulting firm employing around 300 with about 50% exempt level. Seeks math and business majors as benefit analysts. Also seeks experienced personnel in all areas of benefits.

Procedure: Send resume to Human Resources,
310 W. Fourth St., Winston-Salem, NC 27101
(910) 748-1120

GREAT AMERICAN SOUTH, INC.

Profile: Subsidiary of the American Financial Group providing property and casualty insurance employing 230 here. Hires recent grads as marketing and claims trainees. Seeks experienced personnel in accounting/financr, sales, and MIS.

Procedure: Send resume to Human Resources,
3105 Glenwood Ave., Raleigh, NC 27626
(919) 783-1400

GREENSBORO NEWS & RECORD

Profile: Largest daily newspaper in the Triad employing close to 500. Seeks experienced personnel for its editorial and sales staff. Hires recent grads into newspaper management.

Procedure: Send resume to Human Resources,
PO Box 20848, Greensboro, NC 27420
(910) 373-7000

GTE TELEPHONE OPERATIONS

Profile: Triangle telecommunications supplier employing about 2,000 with about 25% exempt level. Hires both recent grads and experienced personnel for engineering, marketing, and technical support. Also seeks experienced personnel for human resources.

Procedure: Send resume to Human Resources,
4100 N. Roxboro Rd., Durham, NC 27704
(919) 471-5000

HARDEES FOOD SYSTEMS, INC.

Profile: Corporate headquarters for this fast-food chain. Does not currently hire recent grads. Seeks experienced personnel primarily in accounting/finance, MIS, and systems analysis.

Procedure: Send resume to Human Resources,
1233 Hardees Blvd., Rocky Mount, NC 27804
(919) 977-2000

HARRIS MILITARY & AEROSPACE

Profile: Designs and manufactures integrated circuits. Employs 100+, mostly exempt level. Seeks both recent grads and experienced personnel for engineering (ME, EE) and production. Not interested in computer science.

Procedure: Send resume to Human Resources,
3026 Cornwallis Rd., RTP, NC 27709
(919) 549-3100

HEWLETT PACKARD CO.

Profile: Provides sales and service for HP computers and electronic devices. Employs about 125, mostly exempt. Rarely hires recent grads. Seeks experienced personnel for sales or service, depending on current needs.

Procedure: Send resume to Human Resources,
2000 Regency Park, Cary, NC 27511
(919) 467-6600

HIGH POINT HOSPITAL

Profile: Largest hospital in High Point employing 1750 with about 33% exempt level. Seeks all medical specialties. Also seeks both recent grads and experienced personnel for accounting/finance and MIS.

Procedure: Send resume to Human Resources,
601 N. Elm St., High Point, NC 27262

(910) 884-8400

HONEYWELL, INC. - ELECTRONIC COMPONENTS
Profile: Electromagnetic and electronics manufacturer employing 200 here with 50% exempt level. Rarely hires recent grads. Seeks experienced personnel for practical and manufacturing engineering.
Procedure: Send resume to Human Resources,
921 Holloway St., Durham, NC 27702
(919) 688-8081

INTERNATIONAL BUSINESS MACHINES (IBM)
Profile: PC manufacturing and network systems hub for the world's largest computer company employing 10,000+ here. Seeks both recent grads and experienced personnel for engineering (all areas), computer science, systems information. Also hires MBAs in marketing, finance, and logistics.
Note: IBM recently announced that it was consolidating its whole PC Division at RTP.
Procedure: Send resume to Human Resources,
3039 Cornwallis Rd., RTP, NC 27709
(919) 543-5221

IEA, INC.
Profile: A private environmental testing lab employing 120 with about 25% exempt level. Hires recent grads in chemistry, biology, and other sciences. Rarely has needs for experienced personnel.
Procedure: Send resume to Human Resources,
3000 Weston Pkwy., Cary, NC 27709
(919) 677-0090

INTEGON INSURANCE
Profile: Local "high risk" insurance provider employing about 1,300 here with about 50% exempt. Hires recent grads for claims positions. Seeks experienced personnel in underwriting and systems analysis.
Procedure: Send resume to Human Resources,
500 W. Fifth St., Winston Salem, NC 27101

(910) 770-2000

INTEGRATED SILICON SYSTEMS, INC.

Profile: An electronic design automation firm employing close to 100, mostly exempt level. Hires a few recent grads with BS or MS degree in computer science or electrical engineering. Seeks experienced personnel in electrical engineering and computer science.

Procedure: Send resume to Human Resources,
PO Box 13665, RTP, NC 27709
(919) 361-5814

JEFFERSON-PILOT LIFE INSURANCE CO.

Profile: Largest life insurer in the Triad employing 500+ here. Hires around 10 recent grads per year in claims, underwriting, accounting/finance, and management. Also seeks experienced programmers and RNs.

Procedure: Send resume to Human Resources,
PO Box 21008, Greensboro, NC 27420
(910) 691-3000

KERR DRUG STORES, INC.

Profile: Headquarters for this regional drugstore employing close to 1,000 here. Hires both recent grads and experienced personnel as pharmacists, managers, and assistant managers.

Procedure: Send resume to Human Resources,
8380 Capital Blvd., Raleigh, NC 27661
(919) 872-5710

KONICA MANUFACTURING

Profile: Producer of color photographic paper employing 330 with about 25% exempt level. Seeks recent grads for engineering and accounting/finance. Seeks experienced personnel for accounting/finance.

Procedure: Send resume to Human Resources,
6900 Konica Dr., Whittsett, NC 27377
(919) 449-8000

KPMG PEAT MARWICK

Profile: One of the world's "Big Six" CPA firms employing about 90
                here, mostly exempt. Hires around 15 MBAs and CPAs
                yearly. Rarely has needs for experienced personnel.
Procedure: Send resume to Recruiter,
                First Union Capital Ctr., Raleigh, NC 27601
                (919) 664-7100

LOWE'S

Profile: Headquarters for this rapidly expanding "home center" chain
                employing 1,500+ here, mostly exempt. Hires both recent
                grads and experienced personnel in engineering, architectural
                drafting, accounting/finance, and MIS.
Procedure: Send resume to Human Resources,
                PO Box 1111, N. Wilkesboro, NC 28656
                (910) 651-4000

LOWE'S FOODS

Profile: This growing supermarket chain employs nearly 3,200
                throughout North Carolina. Hires 7-10 store managers per
                year. Has very little turnover in other professional level areas.
                Not connected with the Lowe's home center chain.
Procedure: Send resume to Human Resources,
                PO Box 24908
                Winston-Salem, NC 27114
                (910) 659-0180

MALLINCKRODT, INC.

Profile: Manufacturer of specialty chemicals employing 300+ with
                about 25% exempt level. Hires recent grads in chemistry and
                chemical engineering. Rarely has needs for experienced
                personnel as they usually promote from within.
Procedure: Send resume to Human Resources,
                8801 Capital Blvd., Raleigh, NC 27604
                (919) 878-2800

MARTIN MARIETTA - TECHNICAL SERVICES

Profile: Provider of computer support to the EPA. Employs nearly
                300 with about 50% exempt level. Rarely hires recent grads
                Hires experienced personnel for programmer analysts,

operations, and system analysts. Also offers a summer co-op program.

Procedure: Send resume to Human Resources,
2710 Wycliff Rd., Raleigh, NC 27622
(919) 783-4550

MCKINNEY & SILVER

Profile: Largest ad agency in Raleigh with 100+ employees, mostly exempt level. Depending on needs, hires both recent grads and experienced personnel into various areas of advertising (creative, media, account management, research).

Procedure: Send resume to Human Resources,
333 Fayetteville St. Mall, Raleigh, NC 27601
(919) 828-0691

MEASUREMENTS GROUP, INC.

Profile: Manufactures stress analysis products used by designers. Employs 450 here with about 25% exempt level. Hires a couple of recent grads per year for mechanical engineering. Rarely has needs for experienced personnel.

Procedure: Send resume to Human Resources,
9517 US Highway 64, Raleigh, NC 27611
(919) 365-3800

MEDIC COMPUTER SYSTEMS

Profile: Software developer and marketer employing 285 with about 50% exempt level. Hires a few recent grads per year for computer science and MIS. Seeks experienced personnel for management and MIS.

Procedure: Send resume to Human Resources,
8601 Six Forks Rd., Suite 300, Raleigh, NC 27615
(919) 842-8102

MEMOREX TELEX CORPORATION

Profile: Developer and manufacturer of computer peripheral devices. Employs 450 with about 33% exempt level. Hires a few recent grads per year for accounting/finance, electrical engineering, and computer science. Also seeks experienced personnel in the same areas.

Procedure: Send resume to Human Resources,
                3301 Terminal Dr., Raleigh, NC 27604
                (919) 250-6000

MITSUBISHI SEMICONDUCTOR AMERICA, INC.

Profile: Manufactures semiconductor chips and employs about 500
                with 33% exempt level. Seeks recent grads for design
                engineers. Also seeks experienced personnel for
                accounting/finance, management, and design engineering.
Procedure: Send resume to Human Resources,
                Three Diamond Lane, Durham, NC 27704
                (919) 479-3333

MOSES H. CONE MEMORIAL HOSPITAL

Profile: Largest hospital in Greensboro employing close to 4,000 with
                about 20% exempt level. Seeks both recent grads and
                experienced personnel in all medical specialties. Also has
                needs for experienced personnel in accounting/finance and
                MIS.
Procedure: Send resume to Human Resources,
                1200 N. Elm St., Greensboro, NC 27401
                (910) 574-7000

MTS SENSORS DIVISION

Profile: Manufacturer of sensors for automation applications.
                Employs 140 here with about 50% exempt level. Rarely hires
                recent grads. Seeks experienced personnel for electrical
                engineering.
Procedure: Send resume to Human Resources,
                3001 Sheldon Dr., Cary, NC 27513
                (919) 677-0100

NATIONAL INSTITUTE OF ENVIRONMENTAL HEALTH

Profile: National agency that measures the effects of environmental
                agents on human health. Employs about 900. Seeks both
                recent grads and experienced personnel in biology,
                biochemistry, chemistry, pharmacy, immunology, biophysics,
                toxicology. Hiring varies according to budget and current
                needs.

Procedure: Applicants must first fill out Standard Form 171 before
               applying.
               For more information, contact Personnel,
               111 TW Alexander Dr., RTP, NC 27709
               (919) 541-3345

NATIONSBANK OF NORTH CAROLINA

Profile: Largest bank in the South employing nearly 2,000 in
               Greensboro. Hires hundreds of recent grads and MBAs
               company-wide each year into various training programs in
               banking (consumer, commercial, mortgage), finance (audit,
               investments), operations. Recently completed construction of
               a High Point facility which will employ nearly 2,000.
Procedure: Hiring done through Charlotte for exempt positions.
               Experienced banking specialists, send resume to Management
               Recruiting,; recent grads or others with no banking
               experience, send to College Recruiting at.
               100 N. Tryon St., Charlotte, NC 28255
               (704) 383-8996 - detailed job information line; 335-2269 -
               fax

NATIONWIDE INSURANCE CO.

Profile: National insurance provider employing 750 here in Raleigh.
               Hires 30+ recent grads per year as claims representatives. Has
               occasional needs for experienced personnel in underwriting,
               claims, and accounting/finance.
Procedure: Send resume to Human Resources,
               4401 Creedmoor Rd., Raleigh, NC 27622
               (919) 781-3322

NORTH CAROLINA BAPTIST HOSPITALS, INC.

Profile: Second largest hospital in the Triad employing 5000+. Seeks
               both recent grads and experienced personnel for
               accounting/finance and management. Also seeks all medical
               specialties. Affiliated with Bowman Gray Medical School.
Procedure: Send resume to Human Resources,
               Medical Center Blvd., Winston-Salem, NC 27157
               (910) 716-4717

NORTH CAROLINA FARM BUREAU MUTUAL INSURANCE

Profile: Local insurance company employing 500+ here in Durham. Hires a few recent grads per year - mostly for underwriting. Seeks experienced personnel in underwriting, claims, and accounting/finance.

Procedure: Send resume to Personnel Manager,
401 W. Chapel Hill St., Durham, NC 27701
(919) 782-1705

NORTH CAROLINA STATE UNIVERSITY

Profile: Public university with an enrollment of 27,000. Employs nearly 2,000 faculty and close to 8,000 support personnel. Seeks recent grads in computer science and accounting/finance. Seeks experienced personnel in accounting/finance and MIS.

Procedure: Applicants must "bid" on available jobs by using the job bid line and submitting their resume. Applicants may bid on 2 jobs per week.
job hotline: (919) 515-3737; job bid line: (919) 515-4309
PO Box 7001, Raleigh, NC 27695

NORTH CAROLINA CENTRAL UNIVERSITY

Profile: Primarily African-American university enrolling close to 6,000 with a support staff of 800+ and a faculty of 300. Seeks both recent grads and experienced personnel in health services, accounting/finance, and MIS.

Procedure: Send resume to Human Resources,
PO Box 19714, Durham, NC 27707
(919) 560-6304

NEWS & OBSERVER PUBLISHING CO.

Profile: Second largest circulation of all North Carolina daily papers with 700 full time employees. Seeks both recent grads and experienced personnel in customer service, circulation MIS, and human resources. For editorial positions, looks for applicants with previous newspaper experience.

Procedure: Send resume to Human Resources,
215 S. McDowell St., Raleigh, NC 27602

(919) 829-4500; job hotline: (919) 549-5100 x5627

NORTHERN TELECOM

Profile: Develops and markets digital switching systems and telephone equipment. Employs about 8,500 with about 50% exempt level. Hires 100+ recent grads and experienced personnel per year - mostly in engineering. Also seeks experienced personnel in accounting/finance and MIS.

Procedure: Send resume to Human Resources,
4001 E. Chapel Hill-Nelson Hwy., RTP, NC 27709
(919) 992-5000

ORGANON TEKNIKA CORPORATION

Profile: Develops and manufactures medical diagnostic tests. Employs about 500 with 50%+ exempt level. Seldom hires recent grads. Seeks experienced personnel in engineering (biochemical, industrial, mechanical), accounting/finance, and MIS.

Procedure: Send resume to Human Resources,
100 Akzo Ave., Durham, NC 27712
(919) 620-2000

OXFORD UNIVERSITY PRESS, INC.

Profile: Distribution center for this international book publisher. Employs 185 with about 50% exempt. Seeks both recent grads and experienced personnel for distribution positions. Also seeks experienced personnel for accounting/finance. Advertisers for openings in Sunday edition of the *News & Observer*.

Procedure: Send resume to Human Resources,
2001 Evans Rd., Cary, NC 27513
(919) 677-0977

PELLING WECK INC.

Profile: Manufacturer of surgical instruments employing 300 here with 50% exempt level. Seeks both recent grads and experienced personnel for R&D, marketing, engineering, and accounting/finance.

Procedure: Send resume to Human Resources,

PO Box 12600, RTP, NC 27709
(919) 544-8000

PENN CORPORATION FINANCIAL, INC.

Profile: Provider of life, accident, and health insurance employing about 500 here in Raleigh. Hires approximately 20 recent grads and experienced personnel per year for claims, underwriting, and accounting/finance.

Procedure: Send resume to Human Resources,
1001 Wade Ave., Raleigh, NC 27605
(919) 834-0751

PEOPLES SECURITY INSURANCE CO.

Profile: Local insurance company employing close to 400 with about 25% exempt level. Seeks recent grads for accounting/finance, insurance (claims, underwriting) and MIS. Rarely has needs for experienced personnel.

Procedure: Send resume to Human Resources,
300 W. Morgan St., Durham, NC 27702
(919) 682-5431

PLANTER'S / LIFE SAVERS

Profile: RJ Reynolds subsidiary and food manufacturer with about 250 exempt level employees. Hires a couple of MBAs per year in either marketing or finance. Also seeks experienced personnel for management and marketing.

Procedure: Send resume to Human Resources,
1100 Reynolds Blvd., Winston-Salem, NC 27102
(910) 741-2000

Q+E SOFTWARE

Profile: A computer database developer employing about 125 with more than 75% exempt level. Hiring about 15 recent grads and experienced personnel per year in computer science. Also offers a co-op program in technical support areas.

Procedure: Send resume to Human Resources,
5540 Centerview Dr., Suite 324, Raleigh, NC 27606
(919) 859-2220

QUINTILES, INC.

Profile: Contract research organization providing clinical trials for pharmaceutical companies. Employs 310 here with about 80% exempt level. Seeks recent grads with masters degree as biostatisticians. Seeks experienced personnel in pharmacy, MIS, and clinical monitoring.

Procedure: Send resume to Human Resources,
PO Box 13979, RTP, NC 27709
(919) 941-2888

RADIAN CORPORATION

Profile: Provider of environmental services employing about 250, mostly exempt. Seeks recent grads for chemistry, environmental engineering, and environmental science. Rarely has needs for experienced personnel.

Procedure: Send resume to Human Resources,
PO Box 13000, RTP, NC 27709
(919) 541-9100

RALPH LAUREN - DISTRIBUTION CENTER

Profile: Distribution center for this international fashion label. Employs close to 500 with about 20% exempt. Hires recent grads into non-exempt warehouse positions with a chance to get promoted. Also seeks experienced personnel for sales, traffic, and logistics.

Procedure: Send resume to Human Resources,
4100 Beechwood Dr., Greensboro, NC 27410
(910) 632-5000

RAYCHEM CORPORATION

Profile: Producer of plant telephone cable accessories employing 650 with about 50% exempt. Seldom hires recent grads. Seeks experienced personnel for accounting/finance, engineering (mechanical, chemical) and operation technicians.

Procedure: Send resume to Human Resources,
PO Box 3000, Fuquay-Varina, NC 27526
(919) 552-3811

RESEARCH TRIANGLE INSTITUTE

Profile: Non-profit contract research organization established by
                UNC, NCSU, and Duke University. Employs 1,500 plus with
                about 50% exempt level. Seeks both recent grads and
                experienced personnel in the physical, life and social sciences.
                Hiring preferences determined by current needs and budget.
Procedure: Send resume to Human Resources,
                PO Box 12194, RTP, NC 27709
                (919) 541-6000

REX HOSPITAL

Profile: Private not-for-profit community hospital employing 3,000
                with about 25% exempt level. Seeks all medical specialties.
                Also hires recent grads and experienced personnel for
                accounting/finance and MIS.
Procedure: Send resume to Human Resources,
                4420 Lake Boone Trail, Raleigh, NC 27607
                (919) 783-3100

RHONE-POULENC AG CO.

Profile: Developer and manufacturer of agricultural products
                employing close to 500. Hires recent grads as research
                associates and for accounting/finance, sales, and MIS.
                Occasionally have needs for experienced sales people, but
                mostly promote from within.
Procedure: Send resume to Human Resources,
                PO Box 12014, RTP, NC 27709
                (919) 549-2000

ROCKET, BURKHEAD, LEWIS, & WINSLOW

Profile: Large ad agency in Raleigh with national accounts employing
                100+, mostly exempt. Sometimes hires recent grads, usually
                into media, PR, traffic, and production departments. Has
                varying needs for experienced personnel in all areas of
                advertising (creative, account management, media).
Procedure: Send resume to Human Resources,
                PO Box 18189, Raleigh, NC 27619
                (919) 848-2600

RJ REYNOLDS TOBACCO CO.

Profile: International producer and marketing of cigarettes and tobacco products employing about 8,500 here. Seeks Phd's for research positions and experienced personnel for its sales positions. Downsizing at the time this book went to press.

Procedure: Send resume to Human Resources,
                401 N. Main St., Winston-Salem, NC 27102
                (910) 741-5000

SARA LEE - CHAMPION PRODUCTS

Profile: Producer and marketer of popular athletic and knit wear employing 450 with about 25% exempt level. Seeks recent grads and MBAs for marketing and analyst positions. Rarely has needs for experienced personnel.

Procedure: Send resume to Human Resources,
                450 Hanes Mill Rd., Winston-Salem, NC 27102
                (910) 519-6500

SARA LEE - FOUNDATIONS

Profile: Foundations and Bali division of Sara Lee Corporation with about 250 exempt level employees. Hires MBAs for accounting/finance and sales. Also seeks experienced personnel in marketing, accounting/finance, and management.

Procedure: Send resume to Human Resources (Foundations),
                PO Box 5100, Winston-Salem, NC 27113
                (910) 519-6053

SARA LEE - HOSIERY DIVISION

Profile: Produces and markets the L'Eggs brand of hosiery. Employs close to 900 with about 25% exempt level. Seeks MBAs for marketing and operations. Occasionally hires experienced personnel for MIS and sales.

Procedure: Send resume to Human Resources (Hosiery Division),
                PO Box 5100, Winston-Salem, NC 27113
                (910) 519-6053

SARA LEE - KNIT PRODUCTS

Profile: SL division that manufactures and markets Hanes underwear. Employs close to 1,200 with about 20% exempt level. Hires MBAs for marketing, accounting/finance, and operations. Has

occasional need for experienced personnel in
acounting/finace, but does little outside hiring.

Procedure: Send resume to Human Resources,
PO Box 5100, Winston-Salem, NC 27113
(910) 519-6053

SAS INSTITUTE

Profile: Computer software developer employing 1,800 with about
75% exempt level. Hires 3-10 recent grads per year for
computer science. Also seeks experienced personnel in
accounitng/finance and MIS.

Procedure: Send resume to Human Resources,
SAS Campus Dr., Cary, NC 27513
(919) 677-8000

SEARS CREDIT CENTRAL

Profile: Provides customer service support for Sears Credit. Employs
750 with about 20% exempt level. Hires recent grads for
customer service and collections positions. Rarely has needs
for experienced personnel.

Procedure: Send resume to Human Resources,
7023 Albert Pick Rd., Greensboro, NC 27409
(910) 665-7300

SIEMENS ENERGY & AUTOMATION, INC.

Profile: Electrical products manufacturer. Subsidiary of Siemens AG.
Employs close to 800 with about 33% exempt level. Hires
recent grads for engineering (electrical, mechanical). Seeks
experienced personnel for engineering and materials
manufacturing.

Procedure: Send resume to Human Resources,
PO Box 29503, Raleigh, NC 27626
(919) 365-6660

SOUTHCHEM, INC.

Profile: Chemicals and solvents manufacturer and distributor
employing 134 with about 50%+ exempt level. Hires a couple
of recent grads per year for its sales trainee program. Seeks
experienced personnel for accounting/finance and sales

Procedure: Send resume to Human Resources,
                 PO Box 1491, Durham, NC 27702
                 (919) 596-0681

SOUTHERN NATIONAL BANK OF NC
Profile: A regional bank employing 400 here at its headquarters with
                 about 50% exempt level. Seeks recent grads and MBAs for its
                 management training programs in commercial, corporate, and
                 retail banking. Seeks experienced personnel in all areas of
                 banking.
                 Note: Souther National recently merged with BB&T of
                 Raleigh.
Procedure: Send resume to Human Resources,
                 PO Box 1215, Winston-Salem, NC 27102-1215
                 (910) 773-7200

STATE EMPLOYEES CREDIT UNION
Profile: Private credit union employing close to 1,700 in the Triangle
                 area with about 25% exempt level. Hires 10+ recent grads per
                 year for its loan officer training program which leads to
                 branch management positions. Rarely has needs for
                 experienced personnel.
Procedure: Send resume to Human Resources,
                 PO Box 27655, Raleigh, NC 27611
                 (919) 839-5000

TRAVELERS INSURANCE COMPANY
Profile: Division of Travelers Insurance responsible for processing
                 medical benefit claims for AT&T. Employs close to 400 with
                 about 25% exempt level. Hires both recent grads and
                 experienced personnel primarily for MIS.
Procedure: Send resume to Human Resources,
                 PO Box 26704, Greensboro, NC 27417
                 (910) 294-3840

TRONE ADVERTISING
Profile: Largest Greensboro advertising firm employing about 80 with
                 75% exempt level. Hires between 2-10 recent grads per year
                 into assistant positions in all areas (media, creative, account

management). Seeks experienced personnel in different areas depending on current needs.

Procedure: Send resume to Human Resources,
PO Box 35565, Greensboro, NC 27425
(910) 886-1622

UNC CENTER FOR PUBLIC TELEVISION

Profile: State supported public broadcaster employing about 200. Most hiring is for the production and engineering divisions. Advertises openings in the Raleigh, Durham, and Chapel Hill newspapers.

Procedure: Applicants must fill out a state employment form
Send resume to Human Resources,
PO Box 14900, RTP, NC 27709
(919) 549-7000

UNIVERSITY OF NORTH CAROLINA AT CHAPEL HILL

Profile: The "flagship" university in the UNC system with an enrollment of 23,000+. Total employment is 8,800 with 3,000 faculty and 1,000 exempt support staff. Rarely hires recent grads but has needs for experienced exempt in accounting/finance, MIS (IBM), molecular biology, and nursing.

Procedure: Applicants must request an employment form either in person or by dialing the job hotline at (919) 910-3200. Send resume to Personnel,
210 Pittsboro St., Chapel Hill, NC 27599
(919) 962-2211

UNIVERSITY OF NORTH CAROLINA AT GREENSBORO

Profile: Four-year public university with an enrollment of 13,000. Total employment is about 1,600 with 660 faculty and 400 exempt support staff. UNCG rarely hires recent grads, but seeks experienced exempt in accounting/finance, administration, and MIS (IBM).

Procedure: Send resume to Personnel,
1000 Spring Garden St., Greensboro, NC 27412
(910) 334-5000

UNIVERSITY OF NORTH CAROLINA HOSPITALS

Profile: Second largest hospital in the Triangle employing 4,000+ with about 750 physicians. Seeks all medical specialties - both entry level and experienced. Hires recent grads into non-exempt administrative positions with a chance for promotion. Also seeks experienced exempt for accounting/finance, human resources, and MIS.

Procedure: Send resume to Human Resources,
Chapel Hill, NC 27514
(919) 966-4131

UNDERWRITERS LABORATORIES, INC.

Profile: Public safety testing firm employing about 450 with approximately 50% exempt level. Seeks both recent grads and experienced exempt for engineering (EE,ME).

Procedure: Send resume to Personnel,
PO Box 13995, RTP, NC 27709
(919) 549-1400; job hotline: (919) 549-5227

UNITED PARCEL SERVICE (UPS)

Profile: National package delivery company employing 2,000+ in the Triangle area. UPS likes to hire entry-level for most positions and then promote from within. A career with UPS in all areas - accounting/finance. management, engineering, human resources - usually starts in non-exempt positions involving package sorting or driving a delivery truck.

Procedure: Call their job hotline at (919) 790-7294 for a listing of current openings. Send resume to Human Resources,
4101 Atlantic Ave., Raleigh, NC 27604
(910) 872-0870

USAIR

Profile: National airline carrier employing 4,000+ here in the Triad. Recent grads usually hired into non-exempt positions - reservations, maintenance - with a chance for promotion. Hires experienced exempt for marketing, computer science, and systems analysts.

Procedure: Send resume to Human Resources,
PO Box 2720, Winston-Salem, NC 27156

(910) 744-4700; job hotline: (910) 661-5341

VETERANS AFFAIRS MEDICAL CENTER
Profile: VA affiliated hospital employing about 2,000 with 475 physician. Seeks all medical specialties, both entry level and experienced. Seeks both recent grads and experienced exempt for accounting/finance and MIS.

Procedure: Send resume to Human Resources,
508 Fulton St., Durham, NC 27704
(919) 286-0411

WAKE COUNTY PUBLIC SCHOOL SYSTEM
Profile: Largest school system in the Triangle employing 9,000 with about 20% exempt level. Rarely hires recent grads, but hires 30+ support staff per year for accounting/finance and MIS.

Procedure: Send resume to Personnel,
PO Box 28041, Raleigh, NC 27611
(919) 850-1600; job hotline: (919) 850-8905

WAKE FOREST UNIVERSITY
Profile: Private university with a Baptist ancestry and a current enrollment of about 5,000 with about 200 faculty and 350 support staff. Rarely hires recent grads, but hires 20-25 experienced exempt for accounting/finance and other support areas.

Profile: Send resume to Human Resources,
PO Box 7226, Winston-Salem, NC 27106
(910) 759-5243

WAKE MEDICAL CENTER
Profile: Largest hospital in Raleigh employing close to 4,000 with 650 physicians. Seeks all medical specialties, both entry-level and experienced exempt. Most recent grads hired into non-exempt support services with a good chance for promotion to exempt positions. Seeks experienced exempt in accounting/finance and MIS.

Procedure: Send resume to Human Resources,
PO Box 14465, Raleigh, NC 27620
(919) 250-8000

WESTINGHOUSE
Profile: Battery manufacturing company employing 845 here with about 20% exempt level. Hires recent grads primarily for engineering (EE, IE, ME). Seeks experienced personnel in chemistry, accounting/finance, engineering, and MIS.

Procedure: Send resume to Human Resources,
PO Box 12159, Winston-Salem, NC 27117
(910) 650-7000

WINSTON-SALEM HEALTH CARE PLAN
Profile: Large HMO provider in Winston-Salem employing 346 with about 30% exempt level. Rarely seeks recent grads. Seeks experienced clinicians in all areas.

Procedure: Send resume to Human Resources,
250 Charlois Blvd., Winston-Salem, NC 27103
(910) 768-4730

WINSTON-SALEM JOURNAL
Profile: The major daily in Winston-Salem employing close to 600. Seeks editorial staff with journalism experience. Hires both recent grads and experienced exempt for accounting/finance and sales. Offers internships in reporting, advertising, and photography.

Procedure: Send resume to Director of Human Resources,
PO Box 3159, Winston-Salem, NC 27102
(910) 727-7211

WINSTON-SALEM / FORSYTH COUNTY SCHOOL SYSTEM
Profile: Largest public school system in Forsyth County employing about 4,000+ with about 25% exempt level. Rarely hires recent grads for support staff positions. Seeks experienced exempt for accounting/fiannce and MIS. Seeks teachers with NC certification.

Procedure: Send resume to Personnel,
PO Box 2513, Winston-Salem, NC 27102
(910) 727-2816

WINSTON-SALEM STATE UNIVERSITY

Profile: Public university with a primarily African-American enrollment, employing 500+ with 150 faculty. For support staff, seeks both recent grads and experienced exempt in accounting/finance and MIS.

Procedure: Send resume to Personnel,
             601 Martin Luther Jr. Dr., Winston-Salem, NC 27110
             (910) 750-2000

WRANGLER CORPORATION

Profile: Clothing manufacturer employing nearly 1,000 in Greensboro with about 33% exempt level. Seeks recent grads for its manufacturing management training program and MIS. Seeks experienced exempt for engineering (ME, manufacturing), accounting/finance, and MIS.

Procedure: Send resume to Human Resources,
             PO Box 21488, Greensboro, NC 27420
             (910) 373-3400

APPENDIX D:

TRIANGLE AND TRIAD PERSONNEL AGENCIES

The following is a list of Triangle and Triad personnel agencies, all members of the North Carolina Association of Personnel Services, followed by their area of specialization.

As I stated in Chapter IV, many good agencies are not members of the association, and so I urge you to follow my suggestions in choosing a personnel agency. Refer back to "Chapter IV, Tool #4: Personnel Agencies."

Cary

ATEK Technical Services
210 Norham Dr.
Cary, NC 27513
(919) 469-2557; fax 4692556
generalist

Dunhill of West Raleigh
975 Walnut St., Suite 260
Cary, NC 27513
(919) 460-9988; fax 460-9931
medical

Rothrock Associates
PO Box 698
Cary, NC 27512-0698
(919) 460-0070; fax 460-0070
engineering

Chapel Hill

Monarch Temporary Services, Inc.
312 W. Franklin St.
Chapel Hill, NC 27514
(919) 942-3212
temps in acctg, fin, legal

Durham

Apple Resources Inc.
3514 University Dr.
Durham, NC 27707
(919) 490-0897; fax 489-3375
engineering, HR, mgt

Ashley Personnel Group, Inc.
3004 Guess Rd., Suite D
Durham, NC 27707
(919) 479-8471; fax 471-3149

Blethen Temporaries, Inc.

One University Place
Suite 160
Durham, NC 27707
(919) 493-8367; fax 493-1650

Careers Unlimited, Inc.
1911 Hillandale Rd.
Suite 1210
Durham, NC 27705
(919) 383-7431; fax 383-5706
generalist

Elite Personnel Services
PO Box 52029
Durham, NC 27717
(919) 493-1449; fax 493-0249
mftg, admin

Selectemps, Inc.
2003 Hwy. 54
Durham, NC 27713
(919) 544-2600; fax 361-2685
generalist temps

Stafco Personnel Services
1000 Park Forty Plaza
Suite 170
Durham, NC 27713
(919) 361-2056; fax 361-2699
generalist

Greensboro

AT&T Services Co.
PO Box 26090
Greensboro, NC 27420
(910) 279-5731; fax 279-3780
tech, data proc temps

Adkins & Associates, Ltd.
PO Box 16062
Greensboro, NC 27416

(910) 378-1261; fax 274-7433
apparel, textiles

Advanced Personnel Resources
20-D Oak Branch Dr.
Greensboro, NC 27407
(910) 855-6664; fax 299-8746
acctg, fin, comp sci, sales

Allen & Associates, Inc.
PO Box 13306
Greensboro, NC 27405
(910) 282-4034; fax 288-5551
data processing

ComputerWurks, Inc.
PO Box 4492
Greensboro, NC 27404
(910) 855-6111; fax 854-3137
comp sci

DATAMASTERS
PO Box 14548
Greensboro, NC 27401
(910) 373-7461; fax 373-1501
comp sci

Express Personnel Services
3716-C Battleground Ave.
Greensboro, NC 27410
(910) 282-7901; fax 282-7903
clerical, HR, materials

Graham & Associates Temps
2100-J W. Cornwallis Dr.
Greensboro, NC 27408
(910) 288-9330; fax 282-8554
clerical, legal data proc, acctg

Gray, Burch, & Co.
PO Box 16832
Greensboro, NC 27416

(910) 854-1474; fax 854-9488
apparel, textiles, printing

JVS Consultants
PO Box 8573
Greensboro, NC 27419
(910) 632-0895; fax 632-9138
biotech, pharm, R&D

LabStaffers, Inc.
PO Box 19422
Greensboro, NC 27416
(910) 316-0045; fax 316-0048
medical, chem, tech temps

Omni Search of NC
PO Box 4174
Greensboro, NC 27404
(910) 368-3362; fax 288-0225
acctg, finance, systems

Shulman & Associates
5411 W. Friendly Ave.
Suite D
Greensboro, NC 27410
(910) 855-7600; fax 855-7779

Staffing Resources of the Triad
PO Box 35048
Greensboro, NC 27425
(910) 668-4400; fax 454-1002
generalist

The Carson Group
PO Box 77035
Greensboro, NC 27417
(910) 294-0334; fax 294-2632
comp sci

The Personnel Center
604 Green Valley Rd.
Suite 303

Greensboro, NC 27408
(910) 855-3654; fax 855-3696
data proc, clerical, admin

High Point

Graham & Associates Temps
1418 Long St.
High Point, NC 27262
(910) 841-2166; fax 841-7274
clerical, admin temps

The Personnel Center, Inc.
803-A N. Main St.
High Point, NC 27262
(910) 841-6644; fax 841-6659
temp generalist

Raleigh

Cline, Jobe, & Associates
PO Box 20286
Raleigh, NC 27619
(919) 872-2880; fax 872-2882

Computer Intelligence, Inc.
7200 Falls of Neuse Rd.
Raleigh, NC 27615
(919) 676-8300; fax 676-8484
data proc, tech, comp sci

Elite Personnel Services
2700 Wycliff Rd.
Suite 100
Raleigh, NC 27607
(919) 881-9000; fax 881-9703
mfg/prod, admin

Fortune Personnel Consultants
PO Box 98388
Raleigh, NC 27624
(910) 848-9929; fax 848-1062

mfg/prod

Greer Personnel Consultants, Inc.
5500 McNeely Dr.
Suite 102
Raleigh, NC 27612
(919) 571-0051; fax 571-7450
admin, legal

Information Systems Professionals
5904 Castlebrook Dr.
Raleigh, NC 27604
(919) 954-9100; fax 954-1947
data proc, telecom, banking

Interim Personnel
6404 Falls of Neuse Rd.
Suite 110
Raleigh, NC 27615
(919) 872-3800; fax 872-9434
medical, home health temps

Ken Walters & Associates
6685 Falls of Neuse Rd.
#208
Raleigh, NC 27615
(919) 847-7772; fax 676-1662
data proc

Legal Personnel Services, Inc.
3724 National Dr.
Suite 121
Raleigh, NC 27615
(919) 787-0049; fax 787-1825
legal

Monarch Technical Services
111 N. Boylan Ave.
Raleigh, NC 27607
(919) 831-4700; fax 831-4714
temp tech, data proc, eng

Phil Ellis Associates, Inc.
PO ox 98925
Raleigh, NC 27624
(919) 676-1061; fax 676-1063
biotech, chem, mfg, pharm

Sports Group Intl.
4700 Six Forks Rd.
Suite 320
Raleigh, NC 27605
(919) 881-8400; fax 783-7598
sales, mark, apparel

The Underwood Group
2840 Plaza Pl.
Suite 211
Raleigh, NC 27612
(919) 782-3024; fax 783-0492
software eng

The Williams Group
1025 Dresser Court
Raleigh, NC 27609
(919) 872-2407; fax 872-1368
exec search

Western Temporary Services
PO Box 20026
Raleigh, NV 27619
(919) 781-5677; fax 781-9070
acctg, sales, secty, tech

Research Triangle Park

R&D Recruiters
PO Box 12509
RTP, NC 27709
(919) 544-7515; fax 544-0162
med, pharm, R&D

Temporary Tech Corporation
PO Box 12509

RTP, NC 27709
(919) 544-7515; fax 544-0162
med, pharm, biotech, R&D

Winston-Salem

AAA Employment of W/S
8025 North Point Blvd.
Suite 108
W-S, NC 27106
(910) 759-2777; fax 759-2778
general

Accounting Personnel of the Triad
4400 Silas Creek Pkwy.
Suite 200
W-S, NC 27104
(910) 768-8188; fax 768-7666
acctg/fin

Alpha Omega Executive Search
PO Box 24013-171
W-S, NC 27114
(910) 659-9001; fax 659-9206
apparel, eng, mfg

Bryant & Co.
PO Box 5171
W-S, NC 27101
(910) 723-7707; fax 750-0152
data proc

Debbie's Temps, Inc.
4431 N. Cherry St.
Suite 50
W-S, NC 27105
(910) 759-9992; fax 759-9255
temp

Employer's Relief, Inc.
3059 Trenwest Dr.
W-S, NC 27103

(910) 760-1622; fax 768-6205
temp

Griffin Services, Inc.
PO Box 11865
W-S, NC 27106
(910) 759-0903; fax 759-0911
general

POPI Temporary Services
514 S. Stratford Rd.
Suite 301
W-S, NC 27103
(910) 727-7600; fax 724-7956
general

Winston Placement, Inc.
PO Box 15366
W-S, NC 27114
(910) 768-4040; fax 765-1865
general

Winston Temporary Service
PO Box 15366
W-S, NC 27113
(910) 768-1830; fax 765-1865
temp

APPENDIX E:

PROFESSIONAL AND TRADE ASSOCIATIONS

Do not underestimate the assistance available through these organizations. Most industries are represented by more than one association, and the following list is only a modicum of the total number of national organizations with Triangle and Triad chapters. If your representative association is not included here, call the national headquarters and ask for the local contacts. Even associations that do not offer direct job assistance are often excellent network sources, especially at their meetings. I have spoken with many people who found their job this way.

Remember that many of the officers and contacts are not paid, but have volunteered their time to help their association. Do not ask to have long-distance phone calls returned and avoid taking up too much of the volunteer's time.

I have included the names of the most recent officers here, but since they are elected for a limited time, they may have changed. If so, ask the past official for the new slate of officers. In case you are not able to locate the new officers, I have also included the phone number of the national headquarters. Call them, ask for "Membership Services," and then inquire the name and phone number of current president for their Raleigh-Durham or Triad chapter.

Also, please let me know of other associations that I have not listed here and who offer job assistance, so that I can include them in future editions. I would also appreciate comments on how useful and successful they are for you.

Alphabetical list of associations and organizations included

American Chemical Society
American Institute of Graphic Arts
American Marketing Association
American Production and Inventory Control System
American Society for Public Administration
American Society for Quality Control
American Society for Training and Development
American Society of Mechanical Engineers
American Society of Women Accountants
Association for Systems Management
Consulting Engineers Council of North Carolina
Institute of Internal Auditors
Instrument Society of America
International Society of Business Communicators
International Foundation of Employee Benefit Plans
National Association of Black Accountants
North Carolina Association of Broadcasters
North Carolina Bankers Association
North Carolina Pharmaceutical Association
North Carolina Society of Accountants
Piedmont Triad Advertising Federation
Professional Engineers of North Carolina
Public Relations Society of America
Society for Human Resource Management
Society for Technical Communication
Triangle Advertising Federation
Women in Communication

AMERICAN CHEMICAL SOCIETY

Membership comprised of chemistry professionals and educators. Current membership stands at about 650. Holds monthly meetings throughout the year excepting the summer. Offers informal job assistance and good networking opportunities. Also publishes a newsletter nine times per year. For more info, contact chairperson K. Wyndham with Greensboro Day School at (910) 288-8590.

AMERICAN INSTITUTE OF GRAPHIC ARTS

Raleigh-Durham chapter has about 100 members comprised of graphic designers and marketing directors. Meets once a month at the NC State Design School. Publishes an AIGA newsletter which occasionally has job opening listings. For membership information, call Julia Zeigler at (919) 554-1771
(212) 807-1990 - National Headquarters

AMERICAN MARKETING ASSOCIATION

Members are from marketing-related backgrounds, mostly research, advertising, planning and analysis. Raleigh-Durham chapter membership totals 150. Meets monthly (Aug.-June) at the Radisson Governor's Inn for dinner. Maintains a job bank which is free to members. Also publishes a newsletter, *Marketing News*, five times a year with job openings and seekers listed. Membership directory published annually. Membership costs $120. For membership information, contact Stuart Munson at (919) 315-3953.
(312) 648-0536 - National Headquarters

AMERICAN PRODUCTION AND INVENTORY CONTROL SOCIETY

Membership comprised of companies and individuals engaged in manufacturing management and inventory control; current membership in Raleigh-Durham is 420. Publishes a monthly newsletter with job openings and job seekers. Meets third Wednesday of the month - except for June, July, and August - at Ballentines at Cameron Village at 6:30 pm. Contact Carolyn Monroe for membership information at (919) 992-5153.
(703) 237-8344 - National Headquarters

AMERICAN SOCIETY FOR PUBLIC ADMINISTRATION

Members are public service and government employees. Does not include job openings or seekers in their newsletter since most government openings are posted elsewhere. Meets quarterly for lunch at announced time and place. Has "Career Talk" during spring meeting to discuss employment opportunities. Contact Greg Dudlica at (919) 360-4211.

293

(202) 393-7878 - National Headquarters

AMERICAN SOCIETY FOR QUALITY CONTROL
Membership comprised of quality control administrators, including governmental, manufacturing, administrative. Raleigh-Durham chapter has about 900 members. They meet monthly, usually at the North Carolina Biotechnology Center on Alexander Dr. in RTP. Publishes a bi-monthly newsletter which occasionally lists job openings and seekers. For membership information, contact Nona Manchester at (919) 990-1155.
(414) 272-8575 - National Headquarters

AMERICAN SOCIETY FOR TRAINING AND DEVELOPMENT
An educational society of personnel trainers and performance managers, both corporate and consultants. **Triad** chapter has 200+ members. Meets the first Tuesday of each month at the Embassy Suites Hotel in Greensboro for lunch. Has a job bank of openings and also has a monthly newsletter.
For more information, contact the Triad ASTD headquarters at (910) 631-6536. For information on the Triangle Chapter, contact their headquarters at (919) 990-2999.
(703) 683-8100 - National Headquarters

AMERICAN SOCIETY OF MECHANICAL ENGINEERS
Eastern North Carolina chapter has 800 regular members and 200 student members. Publishes a monthly newsletter which occasionally includes job openings or seekers. Also offers students a monthly tour of companies in September through May. Meets monthly for dinner - usually at Ballentines at Cameron Village. Job bank maintained at regional office in Dallas; call (800) 445-2388. Contact Bob Simril for membership information at (919) 787-8500.
(212) 705-7722 - National Headquarters

AMERICAN SOCIETY OF WOMEN ACCOUNTANTS
Meets the third Wednesday of each month at 6 pm at the NCSU Faculty Club. Does not have regular meetings in July and August. Offers informal networking opportunities. Also publishes a monthly newsletter. Currently has 45 members. For more information, contact chapter president Beth White as (919) 481-1311.
(800) 326-2163 - National Headquarters.

ASSOCIATION FOR SYSTEMS MANAGEMENT
Membership tends to be more experienced MIS professionals - directors and VP's of MIS and Chief Information Officers of companies. The Triangle

chapter meets for dinner on the second Tuesday of every month (except during the summer) at Sam's Restaurant on Wake Forest Road in Raleigh. No formal assistance, but a good networking opportunity. Monthly newsletter does not include any job openings or seekers.
Contact John Harrison, President, at (919) 954-0355
(216) 243-6900 - National Headquarters

CONSULTING ENGINEERS COUNCIL OF NORTH CAROLINA

Local chapter of the American Consulting Engineers Council with a membership of 146 firms. Publishes a yearly directory of all member companies. Also publishes a monthly newsletter listing job openings. Offers no formal job assistance, but offers good networking opportunities. For more information, contact Becky Beesley at (919) 781-7934,
3301 Women's Club Drive, Suite 123, Raleigh, NC 27612.

INSTITUTE OF INTERNAL AUDITORS

Membership comprised of auditors and accountants in private and public organizations. Grants CIA designation. **Raleigh-Durham chapter** has about 230 members. Meets the second Tuesday night of each month (Sept-May) at the Raleigh Country Club. Publishes a monthly newsletter which lists job openings and seekers. Also maintains a job bank free to members; non-members chargers for use. For membership info, call Johnny Rayfield with the Research Triangle Institute at (919) 541-6454. **Triad chapter** meets the second Monday of each month (Sept-May) for either lunch or dinner. Membership totals about 140. Publishes a monthly newsletter which occasionally lists job openings or seekers. Maintains job bank in Charlotte; call Wayne Keirn at (703) 632-2961 x2510. For membership info, call Martha Rogers at (910) 373-3112.
(407) 830-7600 - National Headquarters

INSTRUMENT SOCIETY OF AMERICA

National headquarters for this organization providing support to instrumentation and control professionals. Nationwide membership totals 50,000. Offers employment abstracts and a resume referral service. ISA also publishes a monthly journal, *InTech*, which lists job openings and seekers. Local chapter has monthly meetings. For more information, contact Vicki Dressen at (919) 990-9282, or write ISA at
PO Box 12277, RTP, NC 27709

INTERNATIONAL SOCIETY OF BUSINESS COMMUNICATORS

Members are professionals in all areas of communications and public relations. Maintains a job placement coordinator to help job seekers. Also

295

published a monthly newsletter, *Communiqué*, that lists both job seekers and openings. For meeting and membership information, contact Nancy Young with Sara Lee (Winston-Salem) at (910) 768-9181.

INT'L FOUNDATION OF EMPLOYEE BENEFIT PLANS
Local chapter is the Carolinas Chapter of Employee Benefits Specialists. Members work in the field of employee benefits. Meets four to five times per year at various sites throughout the Carolinas. Does not offer any formal job assistance, but offers good networking opportunity. Contact Roy Sinclair, President, at (910) 748-1120.
(414) 786-6700 - National Headquarters

NATIONAL ASSOCIATION OF BLACK ACCOUNTANTS
Meetings of the Triangle chapter vary monthly. Publishes a newsletter which sometimes includes job openings and seekers. For information on the next meeting, call their information line at (919) 870-2019.
(301) 474-6222 - National Headquarters.

NORTH CAROLINA ASSOCIATION OF BROADCASTERS
Membership comprised of broadcasting professionals throughout the state. Has a current membership of 151. Does not offer formal job assistance, but does allow for good networking with members. Also publishes a monthly mailing of job openings. Affiliated with National Association of Broadcasters.
For more information, contact Laura Ridgeway at (919) 821-7300,
PO Box 627, Raleigh, NC 27602

NORTH CAROLINA BANKERS ASSOCIATION
Members include banking professionals throughout the state. Does not provide any formal job hunting assistance, but offers a list of employment agencies specializing in banking to its members. Publishes a monthly magazine, *Tarheel Banker*, which sometimes includes job openings and seekers. For more information, contact vice president A.D. Fuqua at (919) 782-6960,
PO Box 30609, Raleigh, NC 27622-0609

NORTH CAROLINA PHARMACEUTICAL ASSOCIATION
Statewide organization with more than 2,500 members representing various pharmaceutical disciplines. Local chapters hold monthly meetings which are a good networking source. Publishes the monthly *Carolina Journal of Pharmacy* which includes both job openings and job seekers. For membership information, contact Cherry Little at (800) 852-7343,

109 Church St., Chapel Hill, NC 27516

NORTH CAROLINA SOCIETY OF ACCOUNTANTS

This organization has 400+ members, mostly CPAs throughout the state. Individual chapters meet monthly. Publishes a monthly newsletter, *The Accountant*, which will publish 2x3 job ads for $75. Also sponsors seminars and professional educational programs. For more information, contact president Wade Powell at (910) 625-1427, 372 Cox Street, Asheboro, NC 27203

PIEDMONT TRIAD ADVERTISING FEDERATION

This local ad club has close to 100 members from both client and agency sides. Meets the 3rd Thursday of each month (except during the summer) for dinner. Meetings are usually held at the Magnolia Manor (Colfax). Also publishes a monthly newsletter. For more information, contact Matt Bowman with WGHPiedmont 8 at (910) 777-1359.

PROFESSIONAL ENGINEERS OF NORTH CAROLINA

Membership totals 2,200 across the state. Membership broken down into chapters throughout North Carolina. No formal job assistance, but offers good networking opportunities. Publishes bimonthly magazine, *The Professional Engineer*, which lists positions available. Individual chapters also publish monthly newsletters. For membership information, call the PENC offices at (919) 872-0683; President: Paul Gordon.

PUBLIC RELATIONS SOCIETY OF AMERICA

The **Triangle** PRSA with 160 members meets monthly on the 4th Thursday for lunch. They also publish a monthly newsletter which includes both job openings and seekers. Also sponsors "Top of Triangle" award ceremony in November. For membership information, contact president Mike McFarland with UNC-CH News Services at (919) 962-2091. The **Triad** chapter with 55 members meets monthly and also puts out a newsletter which occasionally lists job openings and seekers. For membership information, contact Nancy Wolfe with the Wolfe Group at (910) 724-1244.

SOCIETY FOR HUMAN RESOURCE MANAGEMENT

The Raleigh-Durham chapter meets monthly on the third Tuesday - usually at a hotel. Publishes a newsletter for members which lists job openings and seekers. Also maintains a resume referral service for members. For membership information, contact chapter president Roberta Morgan with the SAS Institute at (919) 677-8000
(703) 548-3440 • National Headquarters

SOCIETY FOR TECHNICAL COMMUNICATION

World's largest association of technical communicators. **Raleigh-Durham** chapter meets for dinner the second Tuesday of each month excepting June, July, and August. Publishes a monthly newsletter - the *carolina communiqué* - which lists job openings and seekers. Call president Michael Uhl at (919) 999-6353 for more information. **Triad** chapter meets monthly for dinner and publishes a monthly newsletter - *The Piedmonitor* - which lists job openings in the area. Contact membership information, contact Tom Moriarty at (910) 727-3806

Chapter president: Ron Belcher with AT&T at (910) 727-6263

(703) 522-4114 - National Headquarters

TRIANGLE ADVERTISING FEDERATION

Membership comprised of advertising professionals with agencies, clients, and media. Affiliated with the American Advertising Federation (AAF). Meets the second Wednesday of each month (except for the summer) usually for dinner. Publishes a monthly newsletter, *Broadside*, which occasionally lists job openings. Contact Frank Manson, President, at (919) 832-8200. Membership chair: Jake Lassiter at (919) 829-4642

(202) 898-0089 - National Headquarters.

WOMEN IN COMMUNICATIONS

WIC seeks to improve women's opportunities in the communication professions through professional development and networking. This RTP chapter meets the third Tuesday of each month at the Marriot at RTP for dinner at 6 p.m. and a program at 7 p.m. Maintains a job bank for members. For more information on joining, contact the president, Patty Kinneer with Blue Cross / Blue Shield at (919) 490-4113.

(703) 920-5555 - National Headquarters

APPENDIX F:

GOVERNMENT OFFICES

(1) US. (Federal Agencies)

(2) State of North Carolina

(3) Local counties and cities

GOVERNMENT OFFICES

Federal:

Office of Personnel Management (OPM)
4407 Bland Rd., Suite 200, Raleigh, NC 27609
(919) 790-2822

Largest Federal Agencies in the Triangle:

Department of Labor
12 Davis Dr., RTP, NC 27709
(919) 541-4420

Environmental Protection Agency (EPA)
79 TW Alexander Dr., RTP, NC 27711
(919) 541-2350

US Postal Service
311 New Bern Ave., Raleigh, NC 27611
(919) 831-3661

Federal Aviation Administration (FAA)
2200 Gateway Blvd.
Suite 201
Morrisville, NC 27560
(919) 840-5527

Federal Bureau of Alcohol, Tobacco and Firearms
310 New Bern Ave.
Raleigh, NC 27601
(919) 856-4366

General Accounting Office
PO Box 28165
Raleigh, NC 27611
(919) 829-3500

State of North Carolina

The State Personnel Department publishes weekly a listing of current
openings which it distributes to local libraries and Employment Security
Commissions. Applicants for any position must submit a NC Employment
Application (PD-107) form.

State Controllers Office
> For professional level positions, hires mostly accounting or finance graduates with at least 24 hours of accounting. For information on current openings, call their job hotline at (919) 715-5627. Send application to Personnel Services Division, Phipps Bldg., 3700 Wake Forest Rd., Raleigh, NC 27609-6860.

Auditor State
> Hires accounting and business grads generally with at least 24 hours of accounting. To apply, send resume and application to State Auditor, 300 N. Salisbury St., Raleigh, NC 27603.
> (919) 733-3217

Local:

Raleigh, City of
Profile:
> Government for the City of Raleigh, employing 2,500 with about 25% exempt. Hires 20+ for MIS (IBM), engineering, accounting/finance, and administration.

Procedure:
> To apply for a job, call the job information line at (919) 890-3305 for a list of current openings.
> Send your resume and application to,
> Recruiting Division
> 222 W. Hargett St., Raleigh, NC 27601

Wake County (Raleigh)
Profile:
> Largest of the Triangle county governments employing 3,200 with about 30% exempt level. Most hires for health and human services. Has needs for both entry level and experienced nurses, physical therapists, social workers, and substance abuse counselors.

Procedure:
> To apply, first call their job hotline at (919) 856-6115 to receive a list of their current openings.
> Send resume and application to,
> PO Box 550, Raleigh, NC 27602

Greensboro, City of
Profile:
> Government for the City of Greensboro, employing 2,300 with about 25% exempt. Has extremely low turnover. Possible exempt needs in MIS and engineering positions.

Procedure:
> To apply, call their job hotline at (910) 373-2080 for a listing of current openings.
> Send resume and application to,
> PO Box 3136, Greensboro, NC 27412-3136

Guilford County (Greensboro)

Profile: County government employing 2,400 with about 33% exempt level.
                Most exempt level openings in the social services, health services
                (nurses, physical therapists).
Procedure: Call their job hotline at (910) 373-3600 for a listing of current
                openings.
                Send resume and application to,
                PO Box 3427, Greensboro, NC 27402

Winston-Salem, City of

Profile: Government for City of Winston-Salem, employing about 2,300
                with 20% exempt level. Hires 30+ per year in administration,
                accounting/finance, and MIS (IBM). Occasionally hires recent
                grads.
Procedure: To apply, call their job hotline at (910) 631-6496 for a listing of
                current openings.
                Send resume and application to,
                PO Box 2511, Winston-Salem, NC 27102

Forsyth County (Winston-Salem)

Profile: County government employing 1,600 with about 35% exempt level.
                Hires experienced exempt for MIS (IBM), health care, social work,
                library positions. Small turnover in finance and management
                positions.
Procedure: Call their job hotline at (910) 631-6333
                Send resume and application to,
                Forsyth County Personnel Dept.
                707 Hall of Justice, Winston-Salem, 27101

Durham, City of

Profile: Government for the City of Durham, employing 1,800 with about
                25% exempt level. Hires 20+ experienced exempt per year primarily
                for accounting/finance, engineering, and MIS (IBM).
Procedure: To apply, call their job hotline at (919) 560-4646 x 332-112 for a
                listing of current openings.
                Send resume and application to Human Resources, 101 City Hall
                Place, Durham, NC 27701

Durham County

Profile: County government employing 1,400 with about 40% exempt level.
                Hires about 10 experienced exempt per year - mostly social workers
                and nurses, plus some MIS (IBM).
Procedure: To apply, call their job hotline at (919) 406-9000 for a listing of
                current openings.
                Send resume and application to,
                200 E. Main St., 3rd Fl., Durham, NC 27701

About the authors . . .

STEVE HINES has been involved in personnel recruitment and placement in Atlanta since July, 1970. He is the founder and owner of HINES RECRUITING ASSOCIATES, a professional-level personnel placement service, established in 1975. In addition to THE CAREER SEARCH SYSTEM GUIDES to several cities, he also has written *The Job Hunt* and *Job Networking*. For more information, call (404) 262-7131, or write P O Box 52291, Atlanta, GA 30355.

ADAM BERTOLETT is a reporter and freelance writer living with his wife Suzanne in Winston-Salem, North Carolina.